THE LONE CONFORMIST

THE LONE CONFORMIST

Roy Kerridge

CHATTO & WINDUS

THE HOGARTH PRESS

LONDON

First published in 1984 by
Chatto & Windus. The Hogarth Press
40 William IV Street
London WC2N 4DF

British Library Cataloguing in Publication Data
Kerridge, Roy
The lone conformist.
1. England – Social life and customs – 1945–
I. Title
942.085'6'0924   DA589.4

ISBN 0–7011–2860–7

Typeset by Wyvern Typesetting Ltd, Bristol

Printed in Great Britain by
Redwood Burn Ltd Trowbridge, Wilts

For Ian and Hilary

Contents

AUTHOR'S NOTE AND ACKNOWLEDGEMENTS

Most of the names of people and places in this book are fictitious, but all the incidents described are true. Parts of this book have appeared in the *Spectator*, and are reprinted by kind permission of the Editor.

For their kind help and encouragement, I would like to thank the following individuals: Morrison Halcrow, John Davey, Celia Bassett and her secretarial agency, Laura Smith, The Most Hated Man on the Road, Alexander Chancellor, Charles Moore, Nicholas Bagnall, Sandy Oram and her frogs, Canon Reeves, Michael Wharton, Mr Chisholm, Simon Courtauld, Canon Gundry, the Rev. David Wickert, Father Ian Boyd, Veta, Christopher and Elizabeth Sample of The Gift Box, Deirdre of the Laughter, Mr Templeton, David Sims, Deacon Neville Brown and Family, and finally the staff and interested customers of the Soho Road Library, Handsworth, Birmingham, where this book was completed.

The Bog Cleaner's Lament

Come all you weary bog cleaners, and listen to my song,
It has not many verses, so I won't detain you long.
Whether Gentleman's gentlemen, or whether Ladies maid,
We do not mind our work at all, as long as we are paid.
Don't scorn our clanking buckets nor despise our soapy smell,
For we are loyal to the Crown, and the New Inn as well.

Chorus
So swish the mops together boys, and trip up all our foes,
With broom handles and buckets which we fill with bits of hose.
With mighty swipes, we clean the pipes, and chop up bars of soap,
Throw bleach about! Put paper out! There is no time to mope.
With action fast, we polish brass, and work until all hours
To make the toilets spick and span, 'midst raging wind and showers.

God made the little children, but why I do not know.
They drop the rolls down the bog holes and make them overflow;
Then scatter paper everywhere, just for a merry joke,
And make us bend for each dog end after they've had a smoke.
Now if I was a schoolteacher, a man of mighty brain,
I'd give them Child Psychology with belt and birch and cane.

Now early in the morning-O, we wake up all the tramps,
Some of them poor unfortunates, some cider swilling scamps.
They have a wash to make them posh and totter out the door
Later, we fear, they'll reappear, to sleep upon the floor.
But never mind! Leave cares behind! With rags of soapy flannel
We clean where better men have been, then try another channel.

Now take your trusty scouring brush, some turps and lots of bleach,
And stick your arm into the bowl as far as it can reach.
And when our life on earth is done, and Gabriel makes his call
The bog cleaner can clearly see the writing on the wall.
A marble hall awaits on high, with basins white as snow,
But will the devil pull the chain, and flush us down below?

Chorus

Courtesy of the Ewan McColl Folksong Factory, Stevenage, Herts.

Introduction

I cannot remember the exact day when I could say to myself 'Now I can read!' but it was surely one of the happiest events of my happy childhood.

Denied permission from my well-meaning Communist family to love God, Queen and Country, I would sit yearningly in my grandparents' Middlesex home, poring over the Children's Encyclopaedia. If only it was all true! In the aftermath of the Second World War, the Edwardian world the encyclopaedias portrayed seemed like Paradise, far more so than Communist Russia. At the age of five, I tried to love the Soviet Union but succeeded only in admiring an older Russia of forests, peasant huts painted in floral patterns, witches, fire birds and hump-backed horses. Between the idealism of Arthur Mee and the Russian folk tales my mother read to me at bed-time grew a sweet, sad longing for the past, the roots of my Romantic Conservatism.

Years went by, my grandparents went to their eternal rest, and I reached the age of twenty-two. The Beatles, Harold Wilson and the Comprehensive Schools prepared to engulf what was left of England. No longer a Communist, I felt free to embrace the Vision of England that the teachers at Perrin Road Church of England Primary School had once tried to impress upon me. I had longed in vain to believe them then, held back by the cynical bonds of Communism. Now I could glory in the naïve, hopelessly innocent ideals of chivalry, kindness and Christianity. Ideals I could never live up to, they forever beckoned, a star that showed me the Road to Bethlehem.

Whenever I talked of my ideas to young men of my own age, they would always say the same thing.

'Conformist! You've been brainwashed by the *Daily Express*.'

I have never yet read a copy of the *Daily Express*, so I knew that this couldn't be right. As the nineteen sixties got into their stride, more and more of my friends became intellectuals or 'nonconformists'. It was easy for them to do this, as it merely involved growing long hair and putting on funny clothes. Since leaving school, I had carefully chosen my friends for their non-intellectual qualities. But it was no use. One by one they defected.

'You too!' I would cry, reeling back, as yet another old crony reappeared as a nonconformist, a Bob Dylan record under his arm.

Finally it happened. I was the only conformist left. So I cut myself off from friends of my own age with some heartaches, and became the Lone Conformist, wandering Britain with my faithful plastic bag, containing my treasured personal belongings. These consisted of a pair of pyjamas, a towel, electric razor, shoe polish and brushes, a padlock, a spare pair of shoes and a biro. The latter was the most useful, for it remains the tool of my trade.

Since leaving school at the age of seventeen in 1959, I had partially supported myself by writing essays for the *New Statesman*. Encouraged by this, my grandfather made me an allowance of seven pounds a week, which, thanks to a Trust Fund, was continued for many years after his death. As soon as I succumbed to Conformity, my essays became unsuitable for a socialist weekly. Rejection slips began to mount, but as I wrote novel after unpublished novel in feverish haste, I was protected from starvation by my grandfather's legacy. Years later, I came across this passage in Thomas Love Peacock's *Melincourt*: 'Literature is not the soil in which truth and liberty can flourish, unless their cultivators be independent of the world.'

'How true!' I thought, and blessed my grandfather.

I also discovered an affinity with the writer George Borrow. Like myself, he was very fond of his mother, and lived with her for much of the time between adventures. Peter Simple's 'Way of the World' column in the *Daily Telegraph* became a never-failing source of comfort, reassurance and strength.

Tories and wealth are often supposed to go hand in hand. Yet in the Nineteen-sixties and Seventies, if a writer became a Conservative, he took a Vow of Poverty. Being a Conservative, in the world of the revolutionary arts, was very similar to being a Catholic in late eighteenth-century England. You would not be physically attacked except during a riot, but recognition and a successful career could never be yours.

I continued to write, more than content with my mother's praise, and eventually found a publisher, the Brynmill Press. Founded by two dons at Swansea University, this remarkable firm was rightly praised in Peter Simple's column, my lifeline to sanity in a nonconforming sea of 'progress'.

In the late nineteen-seventies, a glimmering of change, the far-off appearance of the 'New Right', appeared as a pale streak of light on the literary horizon. By now my grandfather's money had run out, I was nearly forty and the present tale had begun. Now read on.

[PART ONE]
Our Village

When seven pounds a week was ten shillings more than a factory worker's wage, I lived on my own in digs all over England, while my mother dwelled in the Sussex village I shall call Pupworth.

'Some goes up and some goes down,' as Brer Rabbit remarked to Brer Fox when the latter jumped in the well bucket. Old Man Inflation rolled on by, a little faster each year, and left my once-proud seven pounds a week a long way behind. Despite having made faces at the local vicar through the church window in my callow *New Statesman* days, I gladly settled down in Pupworth as my mother's jester, companion and resident burden. So if you'll travel back with me to the year 1976, I'll show you around our village.

Suburbia can be a delightful place in which to live, and Pupworth should be visited in April when the cherry trees and magnolias are in bloom. Not so many Aprils ago we had a smithy, where 'T. Daubney, Blacksmith and Farrier' plied his ancient craft of shoeing and making art deco gates in the shape of a quarter sun with rays. Quarter suns, unlike moons, are unknown to science but common on gates.

A number of new residents complained of the noise of Mr Daubney's hammer; and sought to have their rates reduced on the village smith's account. Very hurt, for he was a touchy man, Mr Daubney moved to a Downland village, far from the seaside suburban strip, where he thought he might be appreciated. The forge, a small eighteenth-century building of brick and flint, with a slate roof and a dark, cavernous interior, stood empty on its own beneath the dead elm trees.

At length, a new resident, Mr Miles from Canada, converted the forge into a studio. With an enormous glass window, a new floor and ceiling and the cobbled walls well whitewashed, the building was transformed into a light airy place of easels, canvases and prominent price tags. Soon Mr Miles achieved well-deserved fame, for his paintings of Sussex scenes, with every blade of grass, every stone and even the veins of an ivy leaf, painted in the same meticulous detail, were shown in the Royal Academy. He painted real life views with the unreal clarity of a surrealist painter, a style which he helped to bring into vogue.

Outside his one talent, Mr Miles is considered a bit of a fool. He has a boiled pink face, curly receding hair and frank blue eyes with something shifty about them, as if he were saying 'I, thank God, am a straightforward colonial, honest and above board, not like these complicated hypocritical Southern Englishmen.'

Needless to say, he is a Socialist in a village of Conservatives.

Converting the disused forge to a studio had been no easy task, but it had been carried out to near-perfection by Pupworth's dour, gaunt, tall, shaggy-eyebrowed Guardian Spirit, Mr Saull.

It took me many years to realise the true worth of Mr Saull. Admittedly he was a hard worker, the village stonemason, thatcher, builder, sexton and all-round craftsman, but he seldom spared a smile or a kind word for anyone. He was a tireless parish councillor, parish councilling away behind the scenes with gusto, his casting vote setting a seal on many an improbable scheme which somehow worked out to his advantage.

At Pupworth's Christmas Panto, held in the village hall, Mr Saull is a man transformed. As a jovial Santa, he jokes and plays with delighted children who are often given short shrift when they run up to him in the street a few days later. But it is as a Dame that Mr Saull excels. Bewigged, in skirt, petticoat, rouge and lipstick, he steals the show, dancing, winking and cracking jokes that the children ought not understand. Best of all, he mentions the real names of Pupworthian shopkeepers and others in the audience, in a spirit of ribaldry and non-malicious libel. Roaring, singing, singling out blushing unfortunates and chasing his fellow male actors with leaps and high kicks in apparent matrimonial intent, he recalls the Molly Malone men-women of the old morris-dance plays that long have vanished from the Sussex scene.

Finally I realised that Mr Saull was a Saxon, perhaps the last of the race who doggedly hewed trees, day after winter's day, dug ditches to drain the swampy land, and so built Pupworth. I can imagine the early pagan Mr Saull working till long after dark by rush-light, expecting his slaves to work as hard as he, and cutting a fine figure at the Witan, or whatever passed for a parish council in the First Dark Ages. Obscure points of law would be raised, debated and bent towards Mr Saull's advantage. Puppa, the legendary barbarian who lost his way and founded Pupworth by mistake, might be the nominal ruler, but nothing could be done without Eolderman Saull's consent.

Normally a taciturn man, Anglo-Saxon Saull would worship his gods with flair and emotion, throwing himself into temple rituals and sacrificing sacred mares with aplomb. Our present-day Mr Saull is not only an instinctive actor, but a man who takes the Church very seriously. He casts a protective eye on the gentle, unworldly vicar, shielding his master from the worst facts of Pupworthian daily life.

These facts grow worse and worse as the District Council gains in power. No one in Pupworth can make the smallest alteration to his house or garden without notifying the Council, complete with diagrams and the measurements of everything on the property, even down to the width of the top bar of the art-deco gate.

Mrs Figgins and Mrs Flippance, our chief gossips, inform on anyone who does anything without waiting for council permission. Then rough council workmen burst into the unfortunate household and rip out the new fittings ruthlessly.

Mr Campion the Youth Leader draws a handsome salary, but makes most of his money as a councillor, claiming expenses for everything. In his early days as leader, Mr Campion bullied and persuaded a number of leather-jacketed youths into attending a church service. They clattered in before the first hymn struck up, and sat shuffling and uneasy until the last hymn released them. Far from finding his prestige enhanced, Mr Campion was reviled for his pains, as the old ladies who make up the congregation complained of being frightened out of their wits by the invasion.

Nowadays, however, the old ladies of Pupworth are virtually teen-agers themselves, wearing jeans and medallions and brightly coloured peaked caps. Young people are now admired instead of feared, and, like a see-saw, the youth have deteriorated as the older people have improved. Our current crop of leather-jackets are always being had up for burglary, and not long ago a party of them were caught in a large house at Doddington Furze, where they had raided the cocktail cabinet and were too drunk to leave. The ringleader was a boy who had been sent to grammar school. Before it was abolished, the eleven plus exam was made a matter of Headmaster's Choice. Being virtually a Commu-nist, our primary school headmaster, Mr Churcher, passed only those he deemed to be 'working class', who grew most unsettled at the grammar school.

Mr Campion's Youth Centre is an oddly-shaped modern building. When a young boy died in a car-smash, his father blamed the Centre for introducing him to bad company, as the car was a stolen one. However, the raised school leaving age might have had something to do with it, by turning bright and work-willing youngsters into idle truants. The Centre is now hardly used by young people, but caters for the many Amateur Societies for which Pupworth is justly famous.

Every summer, Pupworth families can be seen waiting near the Youth Centre for the coachloads of French schoolchildren. These summer swallows from across the Channel are yearly invited to Pupworth as lucrative paying guests. Of late it can be noticed that these youngsters speak less and less English, so French education must be in almost the same state as ours.

Pupworth Primary School is a brick and glass modern building whose chief inconvenience is that on a set date in late March the central heating is switched off, even if, as sometimes happens, there are inches of snow outside. Pupworth children are not very nice. Like most

Southern children, from Kent to mid-Devon, the council estate ones have Cockney accents and are spiritual citizens of the Republic of Televisia. In real Cockneyland, the East End of London, the children are nicer altogether. Perhaps it's because city children have everything a modern child could desire, while their country cousins at Pupworth are thwarted. Until lately, no one ever saw a Pupworth child do anything countryish, such as climb a tree, pick a flower or hunt for tiddlers. Fields and streams are at the village edge, but any children there are from London on holiday.

Now the school has a new headmaster, young Pupworth is improving. Short trousers and polite answers are coming back into vogue as I write. Mr Churcher, the former Head, is now running a huge concrete Institution of the Autistic Child in the nearby town, and the Pupworth children are freed from a régime that set them projects on drug addiction. That was *not* what was expected from a Church of England Primary School, as the librarian remarked when the nine-year-olds poured into her premises asking for books on the subject.

Not long ago, when Pupworth was still expanding, the village was a paradise for small builders. Now these are being driven out of business by having to buy expensive 'self employed' stamps.

One builder, Mr Scrace, sold up everything and emigrated to Australia.

'That's the country that rewards hard work!' he said before he left. 'Over here, we just reward the scivers!'

A year later he and his family were back, and he declared that the Australians were all scivers too!

One kind deed of the far-off and inscrutable Council is the refusal of planning permission to build on Pupworth's western border. There pleasant, if rather flat and water-logged, fields meander down to the sea, accompanying the passage of Pupworth's stream, the Crum. Elm trees grow along the lines of ragged hedge, but sad to say, most of these have now succumbed to the Dutch Elm disease, and present a tattered yellowing impression of autumn in spring and summer. The fields fail to reach the beach, as they are halted by the two rows of large houses and private roads known as Doddington Furze. Beneath the waves, beyond the crumbling shore, lies the lost village of Doddington. Fish are supposed to ring the church bells on occasion, when gliding through the belfry, and the last Parish Record of Doddington, in 1820, states that 'the tides having reached the steps of the Vestry and rising daily, it was considered advisable to remove to drier premises.'

A beach of shingle and some rotting weed-covered breakwaters, with a path among sloping lawns makes a fine promenade in sunny weather, along the boundaries of the sunken parish. Dogs race to and fro, and when the tide is out, horses and riders gallop along the shallow sandy pools below the breakwaters, looking splendid in the setting sun. Many different sorts of seagull live here, including the rare Common Gull; and also oyster-catchers, stonechats and cormorants. At night, the lighthouse across the bay gives a quick gleam every few minutes, and middle-aged Pupworthians can recall a time when the Channel was covered in ships.

On the inland side of this walk stand the garish and preposterous monuments to the New Rich, the enormous Mock Tudor, Mock Georgian and Mock Mediterranean houses of the exclusive Doddington Furze Estate. Most of these were built in the nineteen-thirties, and, with old-fashioned snobbery, their inhabitants frown on the 'outsiders' from Pupworth Village. Prams are strictly forbidden on the Estate, as are all hawkers and itinerants. Yet only fifty years ago, the Furze was a gorsey Common, where donkeys raced, ponies grazed and gipsies camped with impunity, sometimes even making furze houses to live in. No furze grows there now, of course.

The inhabitants of Doddington Furze, in their ridiculous wind-swept mansions, seriously suppose that they are living in 'stately homes' in the style of the old nobility. Meanwhile, not a quarter of a mile away, real Georgian manor houses crumble away into ruins beneath the dying elms, the lodge houses standing with shutters awry and windows poked out, all crying for restoration. But the Doddington Furzers heed them not.

To bolster up their belief that they are Gentry, the poor Furzers go in for servants as best as they are able. In the absence of a servant class, they have to be satisfied with an amazing collection of ne'er do wells. Drug addict and Lesbian domestics come and go, semi-lunatic girls look after the baby Furzers while the grown-ups are at cocktail parties, and young Nannies with 'A' levels sneak men friends up into their bedrooms.

Furzers are business people, and these days the business that brings in most money is show business. Curiously, then, the people of Pupworth have a whole galaxy of stars right on their doorstep, each one of which commands a show in its own right, with brassy fanfares of music and mock-working-class catch phrases. None of these celebrities make any impact on Pupworth whatsoever. They do not shop there, speak to anyone there, worship there or sponsor any of the local societies. Lords of the Manor they may fancy themselves, but they would never dream of throwing open their large gardens for fêtes, or of making the acquaintance of anyone outside their Furzey circle.

Far from acting like squires, whom they have never met, the newly-rich Furzers prefer holidays abroad to country pursuits, and sit on beaches rather than on saddles. Boats and trips to tropic seas are what moneyed money is spent on these days, and electric gadgets in gleaming kitchens are displayed with the pride the old rich reserved for richly inlaid cabinets and gilt-framed oil paintings.

At one end of Doddington Furze, near the banks of the Crum, live Mr and Mrs Moore, who were lucky enough to win the Pools. A very jolly, friendly couple, formerly factory workers, they built an extraordinary white house in the form of badly balanced white blocks. White square houses seem to be some peoples' idea of elegance, for quite a poor man is currently building one such for himself and his family, on a piece of waste ground in Pupworth. Anyway, the Moore's creation has a very tall garage with a gigantic folding door, as Mr Moore's delight is a huge scarlet steam-powered fire engine. With bells a-clanging, the happy man drives pell-mell, hell-for-leather around his large paddock in this contraption. The pet sheep hurry out of the way, their bells also ringing, for they are belled at the neck in the old South Down fashion now made superfluous by barbed wire. Other pets of the Moores are rabbits in their stable, a chestnut mare as well, and some white doves in a dove-cote whose squabs are unfortunately eaten by carrion crows. Mrs Moore, a talkative soul, will chatter happily about her pets and her horse-riding daughter, and they even give away free manure to gardeners.

Sad to say, no one at Doddington Furze will speak to the Moores, and the family are now thinking of selling.

Let us now retrace our steps back along the Crum, where swallows dip and wheel in summer, and redshanks paddle in winter. A flint and brick barn stands alone in the fields, its lancet windows reminiscent of the gaps left for archers in medieval castles. The bungalows of Pupworth, where they near the Crum, have deplorable roads around them, for the builders have simply tarmacked over the many lesser streams, tributaries and rivulets. Crum Lane floods in wet weather, and opens out into a basin by the main road, where cars have to plunge and splash their way through. This, before the war, was Pupworth Duck Pond.

North of Pupworth, across a busy road and a railway line, the South Downs stand in all their majesty. Overlooking the village, near the top of one of these Downs, embowered by beech trees, stands a noble manor house. Only three years ago, this was the home of Brigadier and Mrs Dawson and of sundry old retainers. The Brigadier was at one time both President of the Pupworth Preservation Society *and* of the village Conservative Association, and held garden parties in aid of charity. He and his wife died within months of each other, leaving a lot of money to the Salvation Army, the pick of their furniture to a rascally cousin, and the house, garden and what remained of the land to the District Council 'for a charitable purpose'.

Council surveyors declared that it would cost twenty-thousand pounds to modernise the house for institutional purposes, and they decided to pull it down. However, they said, any worthy foundation which pledged to restore the building could have the place rent free for a number of years.

One day the Brigadier's old batman and valet, who was living in the house until his pensioner's council flat was ready, noticed an evil, drunken looking gipsy woman in the garden. Gipsies and others kept raiding the garden for its rare shrubs, flowers and water lilies, which they sold. Quickly, the ex-batman ran outside to chase the intruder away.

To his horror, the raggledy being addressed him in an upper-class voice, and accused *him* of trespassing! He stood open-mouthed in confusion. A younger man appeared, with black greasy hair and a pencil-line moustache.

'It's all right, mother – he's the old fellow the Council told us about', said this lounge-lizardy creature. 'He'll be on his way tomorrow, down into Pupworth. I've just been talking to the Town Hall fellow – our road signs are going up this afternoon.'

Next day, driven to his new home by a Welfare Worker, the batman saw a brand new and very official looking road sign near the turning by the lodge houses: 'Institute of Choreogistics'.

Choreogistics may be a science with which the reader is unfamiliar. Small wonder if this be so, for the new tenants at the Hall, a large theatrical family, have coined the term themselves.

'It is the Science of Movement, in particular of the Dance, and we are the sole pioneers in this field,' they had told the admiring councillors.

A contract was made, and the Institute of Choreogistics came into being. No longer strolling players, but now people of substance, the Cox Family set up house in the old building and made no attempt at repairs. Their prospectus was sent far and wide, and soon a number of pretty, eager young girls had enrolled, mostly those who were too tall, or otherwise unfit, to study as ballerinas. The fees were high, and the pupils had to find accommodation in Pupworth – the Hall being a day-school only. Choreogistics, as any of the Coxes will explain to you, is a system whereby each movement of the human body, whether in dancing or in acting, is represented by a symbol, as in shorthand. Hence an advanced scholar can glance at a sheet of paper covered in dots, dashes and squiggles and either act the part of an epileptic dying in agony, or do the Dance of the Sugar Plum Fairy, as the case may be.

Unluckily for the girls and their forking-up parents, nobody in the world as yet recognises the Choreogistic Code except for the Cox family. So, as yet, Choreogistics has benefitted nobody at all, except the Choreogistic Coxes. For two years, the Coxes did no repairs, but now, with a large class of gullible females and an enormous Arts Council Grant, they are making a start, and the Hall is losing its manorial appearance and character. We at Pupworth should not complain, I suppose, for the girls are an ornament to the village, and pay for their keep all the year round, instead of just in summer like the French schoolchildren. They are driven to and from the village each day by one of the younger Coxes, in a minibus. On the back of this, in large yellow letters, the following slogan is painted: 'In the Dance, All Art is One'; which must surely rank among the Great Meaningless Statements of Our Time.

But I rather miss the Dawsons. Not that I knew them very well, of course, but at the Conservative Association meetings in the Village Hall, it was pleasant to hear them hold forth in their kind-hearted way about 'the poor', little realising that each council house on the Pupworth Estate had not one, but two, shiny cars outside.

The complicated intrigues and feuds of the Council Estate in our village form a separate Pupworth to the flowery suburbia we know so well. As everything needed from Welfare Departments can be obtained by shouting loudly and nastily enough, and as Council Estates tend to look to the nearest Town Hall as a jealously hated combination of master and servant, they have become a people whose normal speech is an outraged shout.

Their strange stories would call for a volume of its own, and each street in our village, in fact, could yield an encyclopaedia. Do come and visit us – our village lies between Portsmouth and Hastings. But, as the reader will find, life's stormy passage was soon to send me, day after day, away from Pupworth to a nearby town with a shiny new Job centre.

Note. For much of the information in the above chapter, we are indebted to our good friends Mrs Flippance and Mrs Figgins. They both share the same cottage, '*Thatch-ways*' and we can't tell which is which.

[PART TWO]
The Summer of Seventy-seven

In early May, 1977, I sat on a rubber chair in the Jobcentre of a sleepy seaside town in Sussex, not far from Pupworth.

'You are now so low that you cannot sink any further', a bright covered pamphlet called 'Unemployed' informed me. My allowance had finally run out altogether.

Everything about the oddly-named Jobcentre was bright and modern, very different from the old grey Labour Exchanges. Nowadays the dole and the jobs are distributed from two different offices, which helps unemployment, as more clerks are needed. I was waiting to see the Occupational Guidance officer and soon my name was called.

My guide proved to be a plump cheerful young lady graduate, with short hair.

'I have studied the form you filled in,' she told me 'and I've found just the job for you, advertised right here. Lavatory attendant, working six days a week, with generous pay. I think that would be ideal for you'.

It could have been worse, so I agreed and was sent off for my interview with the Hygiene Officer, on the other side of town. The guidance lady also left, as it's a circuit-judge type of job, travelling round the county advising people on the most suitable careers open to them.

Her choice for me was based on the way I had filled in my form.

'Question: What sort of job would you (a) *like*, and what sort do you (b) expect to get? Answer: (a) Novelist (b) Lavatory Attendant.'

A white-haired bibulous man, the Hygiene Officer looked at me indulgently. As well he might for no one had applied for the job since it had first been advertised at Easter. In turn, I looked with fascination on the Officer's nose, which was dark red and looked as if the frost had got at it, with black spots and uneven spikes scattered here and there.

In the country-town accents of a ponderous Mayor, the Officer told me that my job would be cleaning, not full-time attending, and that starting at seven, I must clean three mens' lavatories and then go back and do them again, ending in the early afternoon. He was rather vague about it all, but I found that he had told me all he knew. So between us, it was settled how I would spend the Summer of 'Seventy Seven.

Early one morning, therefore, I presented myself at the council depot, an archtypical straggle of brick buildings and concrete parking space, by the railway line, between the gasworks and the Industrial Estate. There I met the Foreman, a short, tough man of incredible energy, who roared a greeting to me from a mouth of yellow teeth. The war had battered him about a bit, and being deaf, he shouted at the top of his voice. Introducing me to Beth, the lady who did the Ladies', he drove us both to the first lavatory, which he cleaned himself in five minutes flat, before taking me on to show me the other two. Whisk, swish, clatter, bang! He worked frenetically, like a man possessed, and I quickly gathered that my job was sweeping, mopping, cleaning basins, wiping porcelain, scattering disinfectant and polishing brass. Admiringly I watched the heroic foreman do all but the last, to new-pin perfection, a vein standing out on his forehead. Later I discovered that he lived in terror of an inspection by the red-nosed Hygiene Officer, Mr Bedford. Why that should be so, nobody could think, as the Officer didn't know where all of the toilets *were* (he once asked me) and plainly wouldn't be able to tell if they hadn't been cleaned for a month. Nor did the Officer know *how* the toilets were cleaned, and could be seen shuddering with nausea at the very thought.

Nevertheless, the poor foreman lived in anxiety, for such was his nature. If a council high-up should criticise or abuse him as some of them did, he would fall ill and collapse in the street, a victim of overwork. I was glad when he finally retired, as it seemed likely he would have dropped dead otherwise. Fancy taking council officials so seriously! Nobody who has not worked for such officials in a humble role could believe how like petty tyrants and bullies some can be, but the Hygiene Officer was an inoffensive man, afraid for his own job, or sinecure. Only when a member of the public complained about a toilet would he emerge from his comfortable office, to pass the rebuke on to the Foreman. Now the Foreman was freed from cleaning the lavatories that I had taken over, and could slow his pace a trifle as he drove his van from village to village over many a mile, on bog-cleaning errands.

Once every lavatory in town had had its personal Attendant, who remained there till evening, but those days of luxury had long passed. Now they were only cleaned and then abandoned to tramps, vandals and the long-suffering public.

Soon on that first day, I met the under-foreman, Ken; two other lady-cleaners, a notorious sciving cleaner who boasted of his fiddles, an old roadsweeper and a young one who was mentally defective. Go to your local public lavatory, for all human life is there.

Ken was a tubby, cheerful man, full of jokes and yet taking his job very seriously. He told me that he sometimes woke up at three in the morning and couldn't go back to sleep for worrying whether the toilets were clean or not. Anxiety and merriment alternated in him, as shown on his very expressive bespectacled face. He reminded me of a hardworking corner-shop grocer, of the sort who gives plenty of 'tick' and then has to worry about bills. It turned out that he had been a master-butcher for years, so I wasn't so far wrong.

On my first day, Ken and the old roadsweeper made a great fuss of the nude 'page three girls' in the *Sun* newspaper. I had always disapproved of pin-up modelling, but the enormous pleasure the pictures evidently gave almost made me change my mind. In workmen's cafés, the pictures, handed round, ogled at and spoken of, clearly brightened the day for thousands of men in humdrum jobs. I was even to see one hardbitten character kissing one of them noisily.

The young roadsweeper came in and joined in the acclaim, which was a bit pathetic, as he was very simple and would never marry. Ken introduced me to him and we shook hands solemnly. Everyone humoured him while he talked about imaginary girlfriends.

Showing me the ropes, Ken explained that I had to sweep up the ilex leaves around the toilet, as the roadsweepers wouldn't work within yards of a Gents. Watching me trying to work, he pointed out that I must always mop along the platform raised just before the porcelain channels.

'Because of the piss', he informed me gravely.

He also surprised me by formally introducing me to the ragged, bearded and incredibly decrepit tramps who slept and washed in the toilets and wandered in and out of them all day. Despite the mess they made, the tramps were popular pets of the bog-cleaning fraternity, who shook their heads and tut-tutted with sympathy over their antics. Soon I got over my incredulity at meeting tramps and ended by feeling quite a benevolent District Officer towards them.

Beth the young, boy-like girl, walked in and out of my Gents' at will. Whenever she could, she cleaned mens' toilets with energy and fervent happiness. Ken took this in his stride.

'What she does in her spare time is no business of mine as long as she does the work well,' he said. However, I don't think Beth did anything very terrible in her spare time. She lived in her council van, very unofficially, and kept blankets, cushions, copies of the *Daily Telegraph* and poetry books inside it.

Rose, the old woman cleaner, was blousy, boozy and sarcastic. According to Beth, she was still drawing maternity benefit for children who had grown up and married, and knowing the sleepy tea-drinking stupor of the town's Welfare, I can well believe it. Whatever money she made, she spent mostly in pubs. Almost collapsing himself with laughter, Ken told me of finding her flat out on a lavatory floor with an empty bottle of whisky in her hand.

'I picked her up and she fell flat on her face!' he gasped, quivering with merriment. 'It's me feet!' she said 'It's me feet!'

June, a young housewife, was my usual 'oppo', a girl whose good looks were combined with a dreadful ferocity, her voice a cross between a whine and a snarl. She worked well and quickly, and then sat on a chair in her doorway on Attendance Duty, which is to say, waiting till going-home time. As I was such a slow worker, I never had any Attending to do, just cleaning. On her attendance chair June seemed to smoulder with seething, sneering vengeance on all mankind. When she spoke, it was always with the air of someone with a grievance who Knows Their Rights. Occasionally she came over and hallooed in the cavern of my Gents', asking if she could borrow a roll of toilet paper or a bar of soap, as supplies were always short. Her complaint was usually that working every weekend kept her away from her family, who missed Sunday outings and Sunday meals.

'Though if my Raymond can't cook 'is own dinner, I *know* there's something wrong,' she once told me darkly.

In the end her husband persuaded her to leave and she was replaced by a tiny skinny wizened old lady like an agile humorous witch. Chipper and sly, with an ear for scandal and not much eye for cleanliness, the new cleaner borrowed not soap, but money and hopped around in the pubs at night, gipsy-like in a headscarf, 'cooeeing' and waving at her acquaintants. But she only arrived at the end of the Summer of 'Seventy Seven.

I didn't see much of the sciving cleaner, as he was always sciving. He made quite an art of this, and explained proudly to me how he left work after an hour, and returned for half an hour before knocking-off time. In the meantime, he set up and dismantled stalls in the market, played fruit machines for hours on end and served in a café. He was a married man, in late middle age, and well able to give today's young people a lesson in worthlessness. If anyone from the council made a swoop to find the toilets neglected, he would just say that he was on his way from one Gents to another at the time, and that vandals must have undone all his sweated-over labour.

Roadsweepers are next on our roll-call, for a sweeper is often a lavatory cleaner promoted, and I was often told that if I stuck it out, and came back season after season, I might one day be a roadsweeper myself. A harsh, wiry little old man in a cloth cap, Ted, was the senior sweeper. His early morning frown, cough and recital of the world's news from the '*Sun*' while washing in a dingy toilet, to me summed up the whole bleak, but sternly-facing-up-to-life atmosphere of going to work in the early early morning. It goes without saying that he arrived on a bicycle and wanted to hang everyone. Tolerant and affable in his curt way to people he actually *met*, he reserved the gallows for dimly imagined beings far away somewhere, who were ruining the country.

'It wants a bloody good war to wake this country up,' he told me. 'Only they daren't do it 'cos it'd be the end of the world,' he added in scorn.

On my first day he alarmed me by saying, as a useful tip, that 'rats are better than mice, as you can chase rats away, but mice always come back.'

However, I was to meet neither rats nor mice on my rounds, though one toilet had at first the traces of rats, as its resident tramp was a messy eater and the crumbs attracted them.

The young roadsweeper was very self-pitying and ineffectual, and should not have been working at all. The dust he swept up got into his eyes and inflamed them, and the work exhausted him, so that he complained all the time. A very emotional lad, he would fly into sudden tempers and run away, sit and sob on kerbstones and lie down on municipal lawns to sleep in the sun. Cricket was his favourite pastime, and some club should have adopted him as a full-time mascot. He had begun in my job and worked his way up, an effective warning to me of the evils of ambition.

I had my own little room in two of the three Gents I worked in, and as it was a cold spring, the sweepers would come in for a warm by the fire from time to time. Council painters also kept their paints and ladders there along with my brooms, mops and housemaid-buckets. The latter must have been named in the pre-war days when the council offices, now hemmed in by modern annexes, had been the local manor house. My starting-off toilet, an ugly dark brick building, was slap on the Squire's old lawn, and overhung by an ilex tree with annoyingly falling leaves that I had to sweep up.

Every pay-day we cleaners and sweepers had to wait on the steps of the manor house for the navy-blue Securicor van with the Alsatian in the back. After twenty minutes or so it would appear and we'd queue up to be handed our money in packets through a gap in the driver's barred window. If it was raining we could wait in the hall, near the Tourist Information desk. I found the whole ritual pleasantly feudal.

'All right?' the old roadsweeper and others would hail me with the ubiquitous greeting, as I hurried along to take my usual seat on the first step. Sometimes I would get my 'all right?' in first, as it's a difficult query to answer, except by a lame 'yes'.

The women were more enthusiastic about meeting and greeting and went away into huddles for womens' talk about their husbands' vasectomies and so on.

'I've had my husband done – have you had *yours* done?'

'Oh yes, I told my Raymond after our fourth, that he'd got to get done. What about you, Marlene?'

On one occasion, a lady lavatory cleaner I did not know went beserk and started screaming at the Securicor man.

'This bloody queuing! This bloody queuing!' she yelled. She was unattractive and gaunt. 'Everyone knows our job, seeing us out here! Everyone knows! Wait till I get them into a union, here! I've told them to join, but they won't listen!'

All the other queuers looked at the woman as if she were mad. Few of them had any time for unions, though many other council employees were members, as it's supposed to take fire to fight fire. If you work for boorish council people who might sack you at any moment, you might as well pay dues to equally dreary unionists who will get you reinstated on the same day. Attending union *meetings*, however, was definitely out.

'He's a Communist!' one of the painters told me, speaking of a well-known portly layabout about town, in a voice of scandalised amusement. 'He belongs to a Trade Union.'

'So do lots of people,' I replied.

'Ah yes, but he goes to *meetings*!' the painter exclaimed, in a shocked voice.

That clinched it, and it turned out that the man *was* a Communist.

Almost every workman I have ever met has been a Conservative without knowing it, as the Conservative Party disguises its real beliefs, so as not to annoy the workers. The idea that socialism and the working class go together is kept up by the *ex* working class, who think that they know better than their parents. The Summer of 'Seventy Seven was a field day for Nature's Conservatives, as it was also the Year of Jubilee, that happy flag-draped summer of Terraced Street Power. I missed all the processions and the excitement, to my regret, as I was confined to the lavatories. Compensation for holiday work came at the end of the season.

'Communist', among my co-workers, was used only as a word of abuse.

'He's not exactly a *Communist*,' Ken observed to me thoughtfully, when talking about the sciving cleaner. 'He's more of a fly-boy.'

At that moment, a council high-up drove by, and Ken made an elaborate mock obeisance after the car. The high-ups were known as 'lords' to all the sweepers and cleaners, who detested them. Imagine a single manor house with over a hundred lords in it, each one greedier than the next, and all promoted within memory from the dregs of the local population! No peasantry in any other age would have stood for it!

Curiously enough, the town had a *real* lord nearby, who owned a great deal of property in the neighbourhood. Most of the streets were named after branches of his family, and everyone I met spoke of him with awe and respect as 'the Earl'. The Queen was loved almost as a fairy-tale figure, a giver of pleasure and holidays and an inspiration for spontaneous street parties, while the Earl was a very real provider of day-to-day gossip. Even a new fence or a cow that bore his patronage was looked on with interest. This lent a strange touch to conversation in workmens' cafés.

Among talk of lorry loads, football and page three of the *Sun* I heard someone say 'The Earl's got a new butler up at the mansion now, an' the old butler's retired and moved into the lodge house.'

By the time the Jubilee flags were up, I felt quite a seasoned lavatory cleaner, and ran panting and gasping towards the bus stop every morning, cutting a swathe through the long grass and sending the flocks of goldfinches scattering, with flashes of yellow wings and nervous twitters. A leaning stick of may bush like a lopsided lollipop, green with pink blossoms, grew to be an old friend, nodded to as I ran.

My bus stop was under an elm tree, by the Pupworth village green, near the council estate. In the soft sunlight of early morning, I would use the battered wooden bus shelter as a 'hide' and gaze through its window at the bright chaffinches and assertive blackbirds squabbling over crumbs scattered around the roots of the tree by the old lady from the electric shop opposite. This elm tree, now dead from the Dutch disease, was then a multi-storey block of flats for wild life. On the top floor lived a large noisy problem-family of rooks, who sometimes flew down and swaggered along the green in shaggy half-mast feathered trousers. Once a dry bone, tossed from a nest on high, fell down and just missed my head. When the disease struck the tree, its demolition squad began at the top, so that the rooks were left as householders carrying on though the green walls were down, their untidy nests visible to all.

Halfway down the tree, in a hole reached through a short corridor of hollow branch, lived an orphan family of five grey squirrels, whose mother had been run over. They were a delight to watch, and grew very tame, sitting up and nibbling peanuts within a few feet of me. As they hopped or ran along the ground, their thistledown tails, soft and see-through, seemed to float up and down behind them. On occasion, they played chasing games on the green like rabbits, running in circles and then suddenly stopping to sit bolt upright, look and listen, their necks craning, backs straight and tails like periscopes. Then if my bus came, they would fly madly to the tree and shoot up the opposite side to where I was standing.

From the bus window, day after day, month upon month, I saw the same wheat fields and the same long line of Scots fir trees with curly branches and black-green blocks of needles. My heart ached to see the green shoots in the fields grow tall and then turn golden, finally to be cut by the combine harvester. Here I was, stuck in the lavatories, when I would rather be among the mountains of Wales. But the squirrels, and people I met, helped me to last the season.

My first toilet of the morning was the gloomy Manor House, so called because it defaced that building. In fact it had gone further, and usurped its title. 'Manor House' now only meant the toilet, while the Georgian building nearby was the 'council offices'. Here at Manor House most of the stores were kept, and that stolen name was painted on the handle of every broom.

Talking of broom handles, nothing was more irritating than when one came off in my hand during vigorous sweeping, as it often did. Banging the pole awkwardly back into the brush-head made me realise how the expression 'flying off the handle' must have originated.

Sponging the walls was much more satisfactory, as the water ran down to form Gothic arches like the icicles in the Thomas Hardy poem.

Often enough, somebody performed a 'number two' mess in the middle of the floor and then trod it all over the place.

'That's what you call "progressive",' the foreman explained to me. 'Here's your rubber gloves – don't ever touch anything with your bare hands'.

Manor House boasted an old weighing machine, chained to the wall. It had been altered to suit decimals, but as the door at the back of the stand that covered the money box was rusty, children robbed it nearly every day. They had prised a slit in the door, and hooked the money out with a stick. This toilet was a favourite playground, and once I found

little girls chalking hopscotch squares into the entrance. I explained
that it was a Gents but they stared at me in blank mockery. Maniacs and
alcoholics had left their marks in the form of felt-tip pictures and
broken bottles, so that it was a most unsuitable place for children.

Schoolboys, drunkards and madmen took their main toll in the late
afternoons, when I was off-duty. In the evenings, the lights went on
automatically and at night the tramps moved into the cubicles and slept
sitting down or curled up on the floor. Most had left just before I came
on duty in the morning.

Just when the robberies from the weighing machine were at their
height, and I was chasing boys out furiously, an unexpected thing
happened. The weighing machine *itself* was stolen, its chain filed
through and only a pale patch on the floor was left to show where it had
once been. Perhaps the boys set it up in another location where they
could take the money out undisturbed. However, the foreman wasn't
worried, as it wasn't a council machine, but only farmed out by a private
firm.

Every cubicle door had a number and in the morning I banged on each
to give the tramps their 'call'. It was a wonder they didn't leave their
shoes outside for polishing.

'Come out number five, your time is up!' I would shout importantly.

One morning, Number Five failed to come out, but only grunted.
The old roadsweeper, sharp-nosed and sharp-eyed, came in coughing
and complaining that the country had grown too soft to birch teenagers,
which it had.

'Stand by to give me a hand,' I asked him, recklessly holding a broom
like a bayonet. 'I've got to get this bloke out of here, so I can clean the
place. All the locks are broken, so he must be holding the door.'

'Don't do that!' cried the martinet, backing away. 'If he attacks you,
there's no compensation. That happened to the bloke last year. Go and
call a copper, that's what you're supposed to do'.

'Come out or I'm going to the police!' I shouted at the jammed door.

'F— me, not the police!' said a voice, and the door flew open to

23

reveal a dishevelled oafish-looking blond-haired youth, with tattooed arms and a sleeping bag.

'Now why didn't you do that before?' I asked. 'If you must sleep in toilets, use the one by the seafront, as I never get there till nearly ten.'

Meekly, he asked me directions and set out for the more peaceful toilet without delay.

Unrest set in halfway through my cleaning-term, as a new young 'lord', Mr Virgo, was appointed head over everyone else. Even the ruby-nosed Hygiene Officer lived in fear of him, and he caused many resignations by his spying and his accusations. Keen as a computer operator, smartly dressed and with a 'this-is-it-basically' nasal voice, the new broom swept away many a cleaner and flew off the handle at the rest. Only the sciving cleaner, the real culprit, escaped without insult and got on famously with the newcomer.

Disguised as a workman in a donkey-jacket, Mr Virgo gave me a surprise visit early one Sunday morning, but luckily I was pottering about as usual. From Manor House, he went to the beach, and accused the girls picking up litter on spiked-sticks of being lazy. They resigned on the spot. All these dramas helped to keep the job interesting.

Angmering Road, my second daily port of call, was altogether a better class of toilet. It was at the back of the club house on the bowling green, and it was locked at night. After cheerless Manor House, the road to the park, lined by trees, always lifted my spirits. That spring a lot of fledgling birds were about, and I could have caught a young crow. On the other side of town, the fire brigade were called to rescue a baby kestrel that had fluttered onto a ledge between two office windows. Opposite the bowling green was a beautiful house with a rose garden and mossy crazy paving that I liked to look at. A between-wars Betjeman-piece, it had latticed windows framed in blue, herringbone brickwork and a built-on conservatory. An agreeable contrast to the cubicles I had to visit.

Brooms and brushes for Angmering Road were stored in the garden shed, a dingy building of wooden beams, motor mowers, rakes and seed catalogues, and smelling of turps and newly cut grass. Here I met the gnarled council gardeners, men from the villages with strong Sussex accents. One of them once put turpentine in the toilets soap dispenser by mistake; just the sort of thing that I usually do, so that I felt most relieved at not being to blame.

French schoolchildren played noisily on the tennis courts, loathed by all as 'foreign students'. Ever since the B.B.C. overdid its homage to the Paris rioters of 'sixty-eight, 'French students' have become folk villains. These particular 'students' were blameless, merry little boys of ten, and their innocent liking for tennis spoke volumes in their favour, but they could do nothing right according to the groundsmen and gardeners. Half-starved by the opportunist families on the council estate who boarded them, they had to spend most of their pocket-money on sweets.

'I like Sussex much better than Paris, where I live,' one small boy told me.

A very small, clean toilet, with no tramps, Angmering Road had a multitude of brass pipes, which I enjoyed polishing. It's a proud feeling, seeing a neglected brown old pipe being brought out into burnished glory. Brass feels grateful, I am sure.

Genial old bowls players praised my work, so that I glowed with my pipes. Master-mind of the bowling league was a hearty old man with a white Sir Francis Drake beard and a resplendent nautical blazer. I liked to think he was an Admiral, and polished away to please him with feudal zeal, mentally likening my toilet to the bottom deck of a battleship.

An aged gentleman with one eye and beautiful manners stopped to admire the brass and gave me a stirring little lecture.

'Young man, I always believe in rewarding industry,' he said. 'You mustn't feel that you are doing menial work. ('No, no') That brass is a credit to you!'

Ah, praise, praise! This fine, splendid old man then took out a cloth bag-purse, tied by string and fumbled in it for a long time.

'Here, I insist!' he pursued, as I modestly refused all gifts. 'I shall give you a shilling. Ah, here we are. It always looks better in silver.'

After some demur, I *did* take it, mercenary swine that I am. So the job had perks!

Another bowler was an old soldier, also with a beard, who was reminded of the First World War by my now frenetic polishing.

'The French used to laugh at us soldiers for all our brass polishing,' he told me. 'Our horse brasses, belts and guns gleamed so brightly that some said they showed the Germans where to bomb us. That's why the French let their brass go rusty.'

You learn something new every day.

My third and last toilet of the day, before returning to Manor House for a final tidy up, was The Seafront. This was a large airy basement, sunny with its glass greenhouse style roof, and much lived in by tramps. It had been opened in the eighteen nineties, and had blue railings round the outside and ornamental ironwork supports to the cisterns. Once a wall had divided it between Ladies and Gents, but now this was down and the Gents had the whole place. The Ladies washroom was locked up, but a retired colonel on holiday single-handedly badgered the council into opening it, to the disgust of Ken and the Foreman. This grand opening and spring cleaning gave me extra work, but it was almost worth it to see the beautiful wash basins adorned with Beardsley-inspired lily leaf designs and every hot tap pouring out steaming water heated by an enormous boiler in my cubby hole room. Tramps moved in at once and Ken feared for the huge mirror, as the Manor House mirror had been smashed by vandals the year before. However, the Seafront mirror is still there, as far as I know. Holidaymakers filled this toilet almost wall to wall, and I worked round them as best as I could. Many came with bottles for the fresh water, and paper towels ran out three times a day. Red tiles on the floor made for pleasant mopping and it was an enjoyable, if exhausting, place to work.

A new ultra-modern Ladies stood next door, surrounded by a

rockery. Often I had to clean in there as well, as its female cleaner had bad toothache now and again. For this occasion I had a special wooden notice, painted black with white lettering that read 'Warning – Male Cleaner in Attendance'.

Charabancs on day outings disgorged their passengers nearby, and on release the holiday makers rushed to the toilets. Great was the shock and rage of the women, as they saw my notice and waited outside in a queue. By the time I had finished, I was the most unpopular man in town. Once a gaggle of middle-aged women, fat and with the vapid stares of Bingo players before the hall opens, tramped past my notice and into the place, expressing no surprise at seeing a man in there. Shocked, I shooed them out.

'Can't you see the notice?' I asked sternly.

'Yes, what does it mean?' their leader asked in a drawn out vacant whine.

On Saturdays, the nearby promenade was full of colourfully dressed holiday-makers, all promenading, and I used to take time off to go and look at them. Sunday School outings took over the shingley beach, one between each set of breakwaters, their banners raised high on posts planted in the pebbles. Each banner bore the name of the street and chapel in London where they had come from. Almost all were from south of the river.

Other secular children (so to speak) changed pound notes into pennies eagerly and played the fruit machines. If it rained, families sat in the shelters and ate sandwiches, watching the gloomy sea.

West Indians came in hired charabancs, and their London-born children, dark-skinned and speaking broad Cockney, were also driven down for the day in vans marked 'Urban Community Aid'. The aiders were mostly shuffling stringy-moustached hippies.

I enjoyed the visits of the cheerful dark-skinned Londoners to my toilet, and once some Trinidad-born boys came down singing 'I want to go to de toilet' over and over, to the tune of 'Stone cold Dead in de Market'.

Two English boys, probably locals, discovered that the Prime Minister's name was Callaghan and spent over an hour in the art-nouveau washroom singing 'Callaghan Man! Callaghan Man!' again and again, in various keys and inflections. After a while, I asked them to sing more quietly and they politely agreed.

In August, the tobacco plants that grew in the park up on ground level began to invade the toilet through a broken pane of glass. Encouraged by the greenhouse atmosphere, they flowered in pinky-mauve blossoms and I called them my hanging garden. A curve of spray from a leaky pipe, later repaired, I referred to as the 'fountain', and with the brass polished like gold, I almost fancied I was living in a stately home.

That was the summer of no wasps. Hover flies took their place instead in large numbers, and all quite harmless. Enormous buff-tailed bumble-bees, attracted by the smell of disinfectant, buzzed in, inhaled and passed out, legs waving feebly. Tenderly I swept them up with a brush and pan and released them in a flower-bed outside. Woodlice I gave the bum's rush, throwing them out into the gardens. Their armadillo shells protected them from harm. Sometimes, however, the effect was spoiled by them landing in a spider's web. Strangely enough, every lavatory woodlouse had one whisker missing, left or right. One day the reason may be told.

A pleasant colleague of mine was a dark-haired young man who spiked rubbish on the beach nearby, and put it into a bag. He often popped into the Seafront toilet to pass the time of day, and I sometimes saw him on the bus. As he dressed in an Army camouflage jacket and slouch hat and carried his spiked stick inside its bag, where it looked a bit like a gun, I thought at first he was a sportsman or blatant poacher. I don't know what tragedy was his, but he had a hole of caved-in flesh in his forehead, the size of a hen's egg. Disconcertingly, he talked to me on the bus about his latest fit, for he was an epileptic and had to take days off now and again. He spoke of these occasions with solemn pride, joked about everything else and once when a particularly mad tramp called Sir John was annoying me, he rushed down and offered to help. Like me, he was a seasonal worker and in the winter the beach looked after itself.

From the foreman I acquired a strong smelling anti-vandal spray, made in California, and so was able to wipe away the felt tip or aerospray slogans of teenage gangs who 'Ruled OK'. In Glasgow I had learned that 'OK' was not a belligerent question, but an affirmation like 'all right'. You would think that ruling O.K. would be a fearful responsibility for boys so young, but actually they never showed up to rule at all, but wrote their slogans in the utmost secrecy at dead of night.

Once and once alone, did I see a slogan being actually written. I was round the corner in the newly-opened washroom, admiring the creeping plants that hung through a crack in the wall and warily eyeing two black tarantula-like spiders that clung head downward to the wall and glowered back at me. However, Ken had told me to clear the lot up, and regretfully I turned back for the broom.

There, before my eyes, were three boys of seventeen or so, rough-looking but flamboyantly dressed in semi-Ted style, their hair brushed back into Rocker Family Crests. With a broad felt-tip nib their leader was writing 'Mombops Kill P-'.

'Hey!' I roared, and all three ran like deer, off in an instant, with me after them. Across the park we raced, round the tennis court, and off towards the Floral Clock.

'Stop! Stop!' I shouted, but on they ran.

Finally, I stopped myself, shook my fist and warned them not to do it again. At this they pulled up, turned round and for the first time took a good look at me. Incredulity shone from three faces, and then, slow as a sunrise an enormous jeer spread over their features. Was *this* the terror they were running from? Three abreast they walked back towards me, shoulders hunched like a scene from '*West Side Story*'. I could almost hear the background music that they too were surely imagining: 'Dom Dom! Dom Dom!'

In the fever of the chase, I had not thought what to do with my quarry when I caught them. Now I would find out, so doing my best to supply a jaunty Irish air as the most suitable mental accompaniment, I sauntered nervously towards them.

'Never write on the walls again!' I warned them sternly. 'Every time you do so, I have to walk all the way back to Manor House to get the stuff to wipe it off! It's a great inconvenience.'

'If you're accusing me of writing on the wall, I'll cut your f-ing throat,' one of the three growled at me.

'It wasn't you. It was *him*,' I answered pointing at the eldest Mombop.

This Mombop, a fresh-faced youth in a blue denim waistcoat with 'Buddy Holly Lives' written on it, looked comically surprised.

'What would Buddy Holly think of such behaviour?' I pursued. 'He'll be turning in his grave, I wouldn't be surprised.'

'If you say I wrote on the wall, I'll cut your throat,' the first youth repeated monotonously.

'It wasn't you, it was him,' I repeated with a weary sigh, and walked away followed by jeers and growly swearwords.

All three walked off towards the seafront, and a moment later a policeman turned up. I pointed them out to him and said that one of them had offered to cut my throat.

'I'll keep an eye on them if I see them again, then. Thanks,' he replied in the mild, half-asleep tone so typical of the town.

Back at Manor House, where I collected the Anti-vandal, I surprised a collection of tough-looking alcoholics standing in the middle of the gangway drinking barley wine from bottles. Among them was the dreadful Sir John and another humorous-looking villain called the Colonel, a tall man with a booming voice and a slave-like girlfriend who stood outside as though tethered to a rail. Two others were there that I had never seen before, and 'bona fide' customers were unable to get through.

'Move along, move along there,' I commanded, pulling at the nearest shoulder.

'Don't ever touch me!' the man hissed, whirling round and staring down into my face with a mad killer's eyes. 'Nobody ever touches me!'

'Oh sorry,' I faltered, observing that he was smartly dressed with short hair, the mark of a criminal.

He strode out, seething.

'Nobody ever touches him,' explained Sir John helpfully. 'He's just out of prison.'

Meanwhile, although the Untouchable had gone, the Colonel was having a row outside with his lady friend, a simple-minded young female vagrant. She ducked when he threw a cider bottle and I had to sweep up the pieces. I wished I could have sprayed them all with Anti-vandal.

Clutching the vital spray, I hurried back to the seafront, along the prom. Whom should I see but the three Mombops, who gave me ironic clenched fist salutes.

'I'll let you off this time,' I told them and they roared in surprise at such effrontery.

Down in the toilet, what did I see? They had returned in my absence and completed their message which now read 'Mombops Kill Punks'.

In a way, it was a relief to see the mystery cleared up and I now knew what Mombops stood for. Such was the Day of the Mombop.

Apart from the punk-killing Mombops, another type of teenager I met were Hell's Angels. In the café where I took unofficial tea-breaks, the local chapter sat near the window, eyeing their row of bikes outside. An ugly lot, tattooed and with swastikas, they seemed to be quite harmless, and old ladies and toddlers stepped round them as if they were furniture and not the dreaded Sussex Hogs.

Rival groups from far away looked much more ferocious, and once a few of them sat on the washbasins in my toilet, combing their locks, smoking and swearing ostentatiously as they chatted among themselves.

'Seen any sign of the 'ogs yet?'

'Nah. That last scrape we was in, in the ditch orf the by-pass, you know, my first thought was for the bike.'

'Naturally – that's what matters. I soon came round, anyway. You've got to have the devil on your side.'

'That's true, yeh – and suicidal tendencies.'

This conversation was perfectly serious, and the remark about the devil came out with passionate feeling.

Later, in the café, an old workman began to grumble to me about the way the resident Hogs slouched around in filthy clothes and gleaming swastikas.

'Did I fight a war for that?' he asked. 'None of them work, they're all on the dole, wearing swastikas and racing other gangs on bikes. It's dreadful. Look at them!'

'I agree,' I said 'but from their point of view, they're not layabouts. They've just got mad ideas, all back to front, that they've learned off telly, films and pop records. People have got to have something to live for, and growing up in modern times, they've hardly heard of patriotism or religion except as jokes, so they make up their own, all wrong.'

'It's not ideas, it's excuses for laziness,' he said with some justification.

Older working people, I've noticed, cannot understand anyone who is ruled by a crazy ideology. This makes teenage behaviour incomprehensible to them, and 'intellectual' behaviour too, particularly that of M.P.s. Every mad egalitarian 'reform' put into practice must have some selfish reason to it, according to this view. Usually, the motive judged in this way, is interpreted as spite or greed, which is why starry-eyed idealists are dismissed as rogues. By taking the side of the Angels, I seem to have digressed my way from the Seafront toilet to the café in the High Street, and as that is a slightly more pleasant place to be, I shall remain there for a while.

As in most such cafés, the owners were a boisterous family from the shores of the Mediterranean. Greek or Italian café owners, I've noticed, are unusually tolerant of Hell's Angels and other ne'er do wells and refer to them quite benevolently as 'the boys'. The café I sat in was no exception to the rule and when a young man returned to 'the caff' after a spell in prison, the owner's wife, who knew very well where he'd been, said 'You look much better since you've been away,' in quite a motherly voice.

An English café owner who put up with drug addicts and layabouts would usually be a crook himself, or someone very shady, not honest and religious like most Italian and Greek café families.

Drug takers kept separate tables to the Sussex Hogs and were quite open about their ways, showing L.S.D. tablets around before the glazed eyes of the shrivelled, skull-faced housewives who sat smoking and staring at their grubby toddlers. The Social Security office was the other drug-rendezvous in town, and the twenty or so young people who had made themselves unemployable gravitated between the two centres.

Conversation at their tables was as bizarre as that of any Hell's Angel:

'Yeah, ole Mick, now 'e was a great guy. We was "tripping" up in 'is flat one day, and 'e says 'Wouldn't it look great if there was fire engines an' all outside, with bells and sirens?' 'E goes out not long after, an' next thing, we 'ears a noise, we looks out, and there *are* fire engines and ladders and all! Turns out 'e's set the 'ouse next door on fire, an' it burned half down! Yeah, a great guy. 'E's still in the mental home now after running along the seafront in the nude.'

'Oh, great, great.'

These druggy young men were not student types, but may once have been clerks. Drugs spread slowly from universities to the working world, part of which they transformed into a non-working world. Along with drugs, American words such as 'great guy' have established themselves among the less intelligent under-forties. Pop music and film fans tend to live in a 'mental America' and to interpret English life in transatlantic terms. This is very catching, and all kinds of important people are talking about the 'inner city' (an American euphemism for Negro quarter) and other Americana as if they existed in England in exactly the same way. Words like 'great' and 'guy' at first sounded affected in English speech, but like 'okay' they soon became naturalised. Now when you hear them in a slurred accent, you at once form a picture in your mind of a dazed young workman with his mouth hanging open, and a dimly brutal outlook on life. This new sort of workman is probably not a drug taker but just wants to feel sophisticated.

Languid young workmen of this sort abounded in the 'caff', and typical phrases became embedded in my mind.

'I fought 'e was a real nice guy, you know, a real nice guy. So when 'e told me that, I fought 'yeah, great, *you* know' But when I got there . . .'

On one side of the town was a large mental home, on the other was an open prison, and 'the caff' seemed to be caught between the two. Mental institutions of various kinds abounded, occupying houses of the long-forgotten wealthy classes, and excursions of lunatics were frequently shepherded into my toilets by hippie-ish attendants who read the wall-slogans with interest. Many ordinary townsfolk had a pronouncedly half-witted look about them, and this pervaded my Summer of 'Seventy Seven with a gentle melancholy. Half the people I met had nowhere to live, and slept in vans, sheds, bushes and lavatories, but this must have 'just been me', stuck on a tramp wavelength.

Seeing a tiny baby in a push chair as yet unable to speak but crying until its mother wearily put a coin in the juke box for the raucous 'pop' that made it happy, gave me a pessimistic insight into the future.

The sweetest babies in the 'caff' by far were the little African ones. Chubby dark faces with big eyes and happy smiles beamed incongruously from heavy woollen bonnets and very British baby-wear. Why, oh why, do not West Africans give up their custom of fostering out babies? Every such foster mother in town was drab, mean and imbecile-looking, with never a smile to match those of their charges.

My favourite baby, a girl, bounced with ecstatic pleasure at the smallest attention. Another almost as charming was a boy who threw things out of his pram, and when I returned them gravely, bowed to me.

Bowing is a West African custom so deeply rooted as to be almost an instinct. A small boy I know in London, who doesn't know his African father or any other African, always bows at anyone who pleases him. The foster mother of the bouncing girl looked positively Neanderthal, surly and lugubrious, with lank black hair, a low jutting brow, vacuous eyes and an equally jutting lower lip. Her own children were no good advertisement. A drearily scornful skull-face fostered the bowing boy. Both would-be mothers sat blankly and bleakly expressionless whenever anyone made a fuss over their charges. Gradually, as the season wore on, the spirits of the babies were broken. Somewhere in London a forty-year-old L.S.E. student from Lagos was congratulating himself on having a wife free to wait on him without having to waste time with children.

A ray of light in the gloom was provided by one of the Hell's Angels, a cripple boy who walked with a stick. He had a golden beard and moustache and a calm genial expression. Able to ride a bike and fond of the pin table, he was also a confidant and sympathiser to anyone in trouble, his heart matching his whiskers. He was one of that rare breed of young man who can talk to a girl and buy her cups of tea without having a lecherous intention.

For that reason a Madonna-like young housewife with a brutal husband poured her heart out to him one day.

'I long so much for children' she said 'but my husband doesn't want any. If only he knew how I felt! My sister's children, when they come over, they *cling* to me, and my heart's too full for words. It's so wonderful to see how a baby grows up and learns things, it really is.'

The boy with the stick solemnly consoled her. It might be wrong to eavesdrop in cafés, but I have an illustrious predecessor in Boswell, who recorded 'a chophouse conversation' every Saturday, more than two hundred years ago.

Sometimes I got into conversations myself. A big young man, of totally wild pagan appearance, long hair with a headband, bare tattooed arms and a Herne the Hunter horn dangling from his neck and resting on his pot belly, proved to have a gentle middle-class accent when spoken to. He was a friend of a rough motor bike boy who had fixed up a brand-new coffin for a side car. Girls who rode around Sussex in a coffin will have something unusual to tell their grandchildren.

Once a harsh-voiced Market Research lady enticed the Hell's Angels and myself into answering a survey for her.

'What social class do you feel you belong to?' she read out from the questionnaire.

At once all the Hogs, noisily and keenly, began to vie with one another to be lower than lower class. They joked a bit, but seemed very serious really.

'I'm working class' – 'Go on, you've never worked' – 'Put lower class then' – 'Yeah, lower class for me too – I'm dead common.'

These remarks pouring out, were stemmed by the researching lady, who chided them and declared that they weren't as low as all that.

'Yeah, I'm common as muck,' the boy with the stick insisted.

No one can understand modern England who does not realise that snobbery has changed over from 'posh' to 'rough' being best. Young people who 'lost caste' over this, by being upper-class and stranded, got back into the swim of things by acting lower than any lower class could be. Hence 'the swinging Sixties' when to be a revolutionary or a drug addict was a miraculous short-cut to the highest ranks of lower class-dom. University 'drop outs' are at least being consistent in their snobbery. Worst of all among New Snobs in my opinion is the young man who hurries his way to the top, scorning those below him, and all the time insisting he's 'working class'.

It would be better of course, if people sought to refine their manners, intellect and tastes, unafraid of the middle or even upper classness this would bring. However, for the past fifteen years the fashionable pose for a young man has been that of an aggressive hooligan on the prowl. Most, I'm glad to say, cannot live up to the hooligan ideal, and like some of the Sussex Hogs, are almost half-decent.

·One day, when the Hogs were well in evidence and I ought to have been working, I sat browsing over a book on the Ashanti War, open at a picture of General Sir Garnet Wolseley. Feeling a pair of eyes on me, I looked up and saw a very nautical little man craning his head to read the book. He was tough, spry and chipper looking, and with his peaked seafarer's cap, white beard, curly moustache and shrewd blue eyes peering through sea-spray eyebrows, he looked a very independent character indeed.

'General Wolseley! My father served under him in the Boer War. Great man! May I have a look, please?'

He turned the pages, stopping at every picture and curling his moustache ends perpetually between finger and thumb. They were like upturned rams' horns. Soon my new friend was telling me all about his life in the Royal Navy and of narrow escapes in war time.

'I don't fear death,' he explained 'as I've been close to it too many times. I'm a Christian! I try and live right, so I've got nothing to fear. I was born near here, at Falham Village, and in those days you really had to work; at seven years old, I would be out planting potatoes. Later I worked over in the chalk pits, burning chalk for lime, in the kilns there, for to put into the fields. When I was twenty I was behind the plough for a farmer on the Earl's estate. Along comes this townie feller one day, a real Cockney. Seeing me there, he laughed at me and told me I didn't know nothing, stuck out in the same bit o' country. This angered me, you know, so I went straight and joined the Royal Navy, long before the last war. I've had a hard life, but a good one, and I'm working yet!'

'What did you like best about the Navy?' I asked him.

'Oh, the children's treats by far. That was at the Navy orphans' home. All year me and my mates would be working on toys and gadgets while we was on board ship. Some very elaborate things we made, electric trains on rails and toy aeroplanes and I don't know what. Finally we'd have leave when the big day came and all go down to the Orphanage with our parcels, to see the children open them. Then there'd be a big tea and fireworks after. I looked forward to that all year.'

We talked on and by and by his keen eyes turned scornfully to the

37

Hell's Angels by the pintable, an unusually dirty matty-haired lot, bristling with swastikas.

'Look at them! I never thought I'd see that in Britain!' he exclaimed, as well he might.

Nevertheless, I felt bound to make half-hearted excuses for the Hogs, as long ago I had (verbally!) championed Rockers against their critics, the Mods. If, instead of fighting in the war, you had been a small child, growing up in its aftermath, you would have thought of a grown up man as a being in short hair, a sports jacket and grey flannel trousers. Then, with rock and roll, came a brand new idea, just as you were growing up yourself. That idea was long hair and fanciful clothes, and it hit Britain like a spiritual bombshell. Short hair had been forever, for young people, and symbolised the Old Order. Long hair and drainpipe trousers seemed impossible but true, and no mere fashion, but a Liberation into a fantasy world where anyone could do anything! Fifties teenagers could not realise that a time had existed when conventional grown-ups looked not like Dennis the Menace's Dad in the *Beano* but as fantastic as any Locarno Lothario or King of the Teds. They imagined they were a new race on the earth, and never realised that clean-cutness was itself a rebellion against the bearded Edwardian dandies who were supposed to have caused the Great War. It was the Kaiser really, but the short-haired and beflannelled youths of the Twenties took it out on anyone with a beard and shouted 'Beaver!' at them. Something must be wrong with an age where every generation thinks itself a new race, but I have pity for those so afflicted, as I was once a sufferer myself.

My new friend, having finished his cup of tea, rose briskly, picked up his rolled-up mackintosh and was soon riding away on an old bone-shaking bicycle. I went back to work leaving a group of housewives gossiping about local women on the game, who supposedly hoarded millions of pounds and sent their unknowing children away to exclusive boarding schools.

After that I was to see the old sailor pedalling around town almost every day. When he came into Manor House toilet and saw me at work, he was very surprised.

'That's my job too!' he said 'I clean the Gents at the big Government Research Centre. Well, I'm blowed!'

'Small world,' I admitted.

'Yes, very true. These public ones must be hard work, full of tramps and vandals. If it was up to me, I'd clear the lot out! This town is too soft! Tramps! They could work if they liked! I'd soon discipline them! "Out," I'd say. Tramps indeed! As for vandals, they should birch them.'

'Perhaps you're right. Is that a mouth organ in your top pocket?'

'It is,' he replied and took it out for a few bars of a hornpipe and then 'a piece of classical'.

Saluting me as a comrade-in-bog, he rode defiantly away. A well-known tramp came out of one of the cubicles.

'Was that the Cap'n I could hear?' he enquired.

'I think so,' I said.

'Tramps! He's a one to talk about tramps! He's been sleeping out for years. They say he sleeps in a hen-house, that's why he cackles so much. I have seen feathers on his coat, but usually he kips down in the Gents where he works. You'll see him in the pub here every Friday night, the worse for drink, dancing and playing the Highland Fling for all he's worth. Yet he scorns the rest of us here. But when the young people act tough, he gets very quiet, believe you me.'

There proved to be a lot of truth in these accusations, but nevertheless the Cap'n was a good old soul, and quite a local character. When I worked on a Sunday morning, I would meet him coming out of the parish church and we would have a drink or a cup of tea together.

Manor House toilet, ill-lit and murky in the cold gloom of a workman's dawn, seems represented in my mind by its patron tramp, Laurence. As soon as he heard me clattering about, he emerged from his sleeping cubicle, banged his arms together to warm up and then doused and spluttered among the cold taps of the wash-basins. He was a big strong stout man in his sixties, dressed always in an enormous overcoat, and with a bush of sandy brown beard and long trailing wisps of hair. Nose and cheeks were pricked pink by frosty nights and his eyes were blue and melancholy, full of sad and ponderous thoughts. Sometimes a grim joviality, eyes narrowing with knowing cunning, illumined his sage-like features, and he reminded me of a Russian moujik in an old story, sometimes drunk and sometimes praying. Like many a moujik, he smelled very badly.

Laurence was recognised by the other tramps as an intellectual, and he knew a great deal about Sussex.

'History is all around you here,' he told me.

His own history was interesting enough, as his father's people had come from Ireland to Somerset and settled there for a generation. When Arundel Castle was restored and rebuilt in Gothic style, Laurence's grandfather, a stonemason, came to Sussex along with loads of Somerset stone, and was installed with his family in a tall tower in the ducal park.

'My father was the castle mason too, and I remember my mother throwing food to the deer from the tower window,' he told me slowly, deep in thought. 'Bah, but he was a brutal man, my father! Rough, very rough, but a good workman. The castle had been repaired with Somerset stone inside and York outside, and my father knew every stone. But he shouldn't have treated my mother like that. Well, there were many other families came from far and wide to work on the castle and their descendents live there yet. To my mind, there's something *Scottish* about Arundel. Plenty of Pettigrews live there – I think one had a shop in the High Street – and there are Scottish field names in the country outside. I go over and see the place when I'm around that part, staying in the Spike at Brighton. That Spike's in the hospital, and it's one of the old sort, that only lets you stay three nights!'

Fascinated, I would let my mop move in slower and slower circles until I was leaning on it, listening to Laurence's tales of his first job at fourteen as a brick worker, and his subsequent career as a farm hand in North Dakota, where he went to live for a while.

'When the Indians got drunk they used to *dance*!' he exclaimed in wonderment.

Every now and then, Laurence would beg from the town convent, which gave food and sometimes money to tramps. The nuns even gave a room to a fierce, white-haired old man called Snowy, who walked rapidly and doggedly from town to town, his head down, filled with intense thoughts of old steam railways, his avowed 'passion'. Another most unworthy tramp called Jock collected packets of sandwiches from the Sisters, but Laurence, although he was a sincere Catholic, got next to nothing, or so he said.

'It's that new Mother Superior!' he complained in a shocked voice. 'She's always trying to save food by turning away the men on the road. What kind of a Christian do you call that? Bah! They're *worse*, the nuns are *worse* than those who don't believe in God. Some people don't believe in God, you know.'

'More fool them,' I replied with schoolmarmly briskness, as I feared he was giving in to Doubt. With no Heaven to look forward to, his case would be bleak indeed.

'Yes, it's a hard life for the men on the road. All kind of things happen – there's a lot of mental illness on the road. It's the wars, you know. I must be mad. I must be ma-aa-ad to live like this.'

'Can't you find anywhere to stay?'

'Yes, I can, but I won't do it. I did have my own shop. My wife, she was a German girl, she ran away. Before that, my son, ever since he got a hit on the head, began to steal. I paid back every penny. But when my wife left, I would *not* lie down in a house any more. Ah, what is love? Love can be a blessing, but for some, you know, love can be a curse'.

When Laurence got like this, I would steer the conversation back to the gossip of the road. To listen to tramps talking about 'the road' you would imagine they were perpetually on the move from Plymouth to Dover, Scapa Flow to Beachy Head. Actually, this fabled 'road' was usually the highway between the Seafront and Manor House toilets, the convent and the off-licence.

Off-licences were Laurence's weak point, for he liked a bottle of

Guinness a day. This would not be unreasonable, except that he literally cracked his bottles by putting the metal caps in the hinge of a toilet door, shutting the door and pulling. Instead of the cap, the whole neck of the bottle came off as often as not, and broken glass and stout would spoil my nice clean floor. However, he was always very apologetic about this.

The same wild, rapacious children who battened on the weighing machine, followed Laurence about the town at a cautious distance, like pariah dogs. They were hoping to steal something out of the old potato sack he carried his belongings about in. Like a weary Santa Claus, Laurence was never without his sack, but unlike that saint, he didn't want children poking about in it. In the end they stole it, and after an interval of sacklessness, he reappeared incongruously clutching a trendy shoulder bag marked 'Ohio State Penitentiary'. Before that happened, I once agreed to lock his belongings in my cupboard. Seeing him come out without them the children's eyes gleamed with weasel-like greed, and a spasm of excitement seemed to run through them. As I left for Angmering Road, I saw them rush into Manor House to ransack every cubicle for Laurence's pitiful bits of rag and crust, scavenged from litter bins and places where people threw bread to the birds. Devilment was their only motive – they even looked in the toilet dustbin.

Sometimes Laurence grew too lugubrious for my liking, crying aloud like King Lear, bemoaning his lost wife, the two hundred pounds he paid back for his son and the hopeless nature of life and love.

On these occasions I would get him to play 'I Spy with My Little Eye' until he felt better.

Among the other tramps, Laurence was less melancholic, as they talked football and rolled dog-ends with stubby fingers. He was a well-liked man as far as his rather ironic colleagues were capable of liking anyone.

When talking of his war experiences, Laurence took an anti-Churchillian line. Although his descriptions of dukes and Red Indians suggested a love of tradition, he often professed to be a

Communist. This interested and appealed to the other tramps, for when you have nothing at all, you are naturally attracted by the idea of sharing. Inflamed by Communism, they once began to run down England.

'England isn't such a bad place!' I felt moved to chime in. 'At least we've all got a roof over . . . oh, sorry!'

They understood, and looked tactful.

Another Manor House tramp was Tom, a little rat-faced man with a red nose, ginger beard and gooseberry eyes. He felt himself to be a cut above the others, as he came from that interesting world where the migrant labourer, as he gets older, fades into the tramp. Sometimes known as 'Scouse', Tom was a Liverpool Irishman, and many Irish workmen, I've noticed, regard a roof over their heads as a rather expensive luxury. From the first, Tom was terribly anxious about his suitcase, which he hid in shrubberies and lurked around all day staring at. At his request, I locked it in the meter cupboard and kept it there all season, which made *me* anxious instead, as I knew the Foreman wouldn't approve. But it was never discovered.

Holding himself aloof from the other tramps, Tom made me his confidant. He had been a coal miner and a sailor in his time, and had the Liverpudlian's satirical outlook on life, endlessly amused by the foibles of the English and Irish. As he recounted the gossip of the road and the toilets, a grin of wonder dispelled the furtive, bitter outlines of his face, and his eyes bulged with mock horrified surprise at the follies and hypocrisies of trampkind.

However, he did not regard himself as part of the normal world, as when he found a job, and Ken the under-foreman asked him about it, he replied with a long rigmarole of lies and nonsense.

'Never let these people know your business,' he warned me afterwards. I think he regarded me as a superior tramp like himself.

Ken and he regarded one another with distaste. Laurence was Ken's favourite tramp, the one he introduced me to on my first day, and after that the gentlemanly Commander Williams of the Seafront.

Tom's job was on the turnstile at the Hall of Mirrors in the gloomy indoor funfair. Sometimes I would drop in and see him at work, handing out tickets rapidly and dropping money into a tin, a system that allowed no fiddling. However, his suitcase continued in my care, his home remained a lavatory and his clothes stayed unchanged and scruffy looking, with two coats on at once.

One day, he sold tickets to some well-dressed confident Asian youths, and then turned to me and said 'It was marvellous out in India! The wogs was everywhere, waiting on you for pennies, doing anything you asked them. Over here, they want to be *equal*!'

At this thought, he laughed incredulously and bent to pick up a dog end.

Most of the townpeople seemed offended at the mere *sight* of a coloured person, who would be instantly assumed to be drawing a huge dole. Near Manor House, where the genteel Quakers had their headquarters, these attitudes were reversed, and coloured people were extravagantly idealised.

A most notorious tramp was Jock, who had become a legend in Laurence's time. In fact Laurence complained and ranted about him for weeks, always beginning 'What kind of man is that?' and then answering his own question.

'He's the most hated man on the road! The most hated man! He steals anything left around and sells it to Irish labourers! He steals pick axes and tools from holes in the road when the men aren't looking, and sells them to buy drink. Once he stole a giro cheque from a man out there by the Jobcentre and when the man said he'd lost it, Jock bought him a drink to cheer him up out of the stolen money! Mind you, he's not a Christian. He's a Glasgow Jew. Yet he goes into churches time and again and robs the poor box, and then as he goes out, he says to anyone there, in a loud voice, that he'll pray for their souls! What kind of man is that? What kind of man is that who'd steal from a church? He's the Most Hated Man on the Road! He's a – bah, he's a mumper.'

Naturally, all this made me curious. One day Tom told me that the elusive Jock was in Manor House, so with a carefully assumed nonchalent air, I shuffled in expecting to see something spectacular in wickedness. Laurence stood munching a sandwich with an air of reserve, while the Most Hated Man sat on the metal litter bin, bending it, as he waved a packet of food about to help illustrate the point of a story. When Laurence had done the honours, the Most Hated Man greeted me expansively. He was one of the most jovial men I had ever met, his face forever creased into an enormous grin, his eyes full of humour behind the horn-rims and his silver hair swept back to reveal an intellectual slope of forehead. With all this went the swagger of a rascal, the loud voice of a Scot and the itinerant's shabby mackintosh with a bottle in the pocket.

Never did a tramp give me less to complain about than Dishonest Jock. He had a way with the nuns at the convent and nearly every day he left me a packet of sandwiches he had scrounged for Laurence, for whom he seemed concerned. Laurence ate the sandwiches, but scandalised beyond all measure at the poor-box robberies, continued to refer to Jock as The Most Hated Man on the Road.

Other tramps, with various quirks, drifted vaguely into the edge of my lavatorial world. I never found out who drank the surgical spirits from the empty bottles I found in Number Four cubicle. Sometimes some milky fluid was left, diluted with water.

A mournful harassed man, with slicked back hair and the ubiquitous long overcoat, was said to be on the run from a maintenance order. He spent a lot of time washing. One day, Elvis Presley died and I commented on the fact.

'Who's Elvis Presley?' he asked, and then thought hard. 'Mind you I don't know a great deal about football.'

I was sorry to hear about Elvis, a strange man, first hailed as a sinner, but ending up almost as a saint for his British fanclub members. Most of these respectable young people, who meet every Easter at the Cheltenham Y.M.C.A., regard the late singer as a Jesus-figure, as a dip into their magazine *Elvis Monthly* will confirm. 'The King', as they call him, became increasingly fond of hymns and gospel music as he neared his end and his good influence has a real religious source.

Another great washer was a tall dark-haired young man with a slight Scottish accent. He seemed morose and embittered and the other tramps agreed that he was 'slightly mental'. He washed his clothes as well as himself, to my surprise.

'A clean shirt again today, I see!' I exclaimed admiringly.

'You've got to be clean when you're living rough,' he replied, glaring and speaking with self-pitying emphasis. 'Ah'm writing to the papers about it'.

'Whatever about?' I asked, almost laughing.

'My degradation,' he answered solemnly. 'They've got to do something about my degradation.'

As he was young and strong, I couldn't take his complaints very seriously, but the editor of the local paper did. Soon the degraded one made headlines, to the amusement of the older tramps. There he was, with a big photo of himself crouching in the ruined house he lived in, and accusing the local council of letting him 'live on fresh air'.

Sure enough, the Welfare took him up at once after this, and soon he had a room and was swanking about the town in a new suit with a girl on his arm, not speaking to former associates.

'Why don't you *all* go to the newspaper office?' I asked the older tramps excitedly, but they just laughed. So I went to the paper for them, but the office girl just laughed too.

Disgruntled, I took a long tea break and visited the Social Services Office. A hard-faced young Welfare girl slid back a ticket-office door and poked her head out of a hatch at my knock. I explained about my tramps and their hardships.

'Where's the dosshouse for the tramps?' she called sharply over her shoulder to someone. Soon she gave me the address of the three-night spike where Laurence sometimes stayed.

'Tell them to go there,' she said. 'Or they can come here first, if they like.'

'Well, they're mostly mental in some way, and won't take any notice.'

'Oh well, if they choose to live like that, it's their own affair, thank you.'

A lot of tramp-hood seems to be caused by the Rent Act, which has abolished 'digs', as it's too risky to take in lodgers who can't be evicted. Migrant labourers between jobs are now having to sleep out, and you can't get Assistance (or Social Security) without an address, or as often as not, an address without Assistance. Those who *do* let their rooms are often on Assistance themselves so they cannot allow the tenants to claim also, as that would forfeit *their* claim. Tom told me this, and I heard the same from young people in digs. At one time, migrant labourers adopted some favourite town when they got older, and stayed as permanent workmen. Since the Rent Act was passed, they have been entrampified, so to speak. But as I told the Welfare, most of the tramps were a bit unhinged, due to different personal tragedies. Some social workers actually tell homeless people to become squatters, but in this town they weren't sophisticated enough to encourage crime.

'Come on out!' I called unfeelingly, one morning, as I made ready to clean Number Three cubicle, which had been locked for half an hour.

There was no answer. Liverpool Tom looked on with shrewd curiosity, reminding me of a bedraggled magpie. I knocked hard and a thick deep East End voice shouted, 'Blimey, wait a minute!'

'A Cockney,' I exclaimed, and Tom nodded sagaciously.

A moment later the bolt clicked back, I opened the door and there, sitting fully clothed on the bowl was a big strong old man in a muffler with large hands and a face like a knobbly King Edward potato with half-shut eyes. The potato opened its mouth and asked if it might not stay a little while longer.

'Certainly not!' I replied briskly. 'You can move on to Number Five while I do this one. Ones that I've cleaned are reserved for the public.'

The Cockney soon got used to this nomadic existence, and every morning from then on, I moved him from number to number, as if he were a counter in a board game. Observing this, a member of the public told me that in the East End itself he had tried to use a toilet but found every compartment with its resident tramp. He called the attendant, who in turn called a policeman. While the policeman stood there to guard him, the attendant produced a bicycle pump full of water and squirted some into every cubicle. With much clattering and swearing, all the doors burst open and a whole row of tramps rushed from the building neither looking to left or right and pelted out into the streets. I never had to use such drastic measures, as my tramps were more obedient.

Before long, the Cockney became a well-known local figure, very loyal to The Crown; where he wiped tables and collected glasses. Here he met the Cap'n, my seafaring friend, and as he had been in the Royal Navy too, they had many an animated discussion on the rival merits of eight-inch guns and six-inch guns. In the end, they both agreed that eight-inch guns were best.

However, when I was passing the pub one lunchtime, I saw a crowd gathered and the poor old Cockney came out on a stretcher, with a cut on his brown bald potato head. As the ambulance drove away, the Cap'n came out wiping beer from his whiskers and looking irritable.

'What happened to the Cockney?' I asked.

'Oh him! He fell over, that's all. I've no sympathy for him and I'll tell you why. 'Cause he's lazy, that's why.'

Perhaps the Cockney's accident, which did not seem too severe, was the means of him finding a roof over his head, for I never saw him again in the cubicles.

When Ken first showed me the spacious glass-roofed underground Seafront toilet, he paused at the top of the steps to wave to a small bearded man sitting under a shelter near the beach. The man raised a hand benevolently.

'That's Commander Williams,' he told me. 'Very nice chap, that, though he must be mentally ill. He sleeps down in this one, and he's a terror for dropping matches, but he'll give you no real trouble. He used to be a well-known playboy in his way, since he left the Navy. He was very wealthy with a big house and land, and a yacht, but when his mother died he went like this. For years his friends tried to help him, and put him up and got him treatment, but he always comes back here. It's a sad case really'.

The gentleman-tramp is such a stock figure in television comedies that I was surprised to find one in real life, and was curious to meet him. At first he was shy, and the only trace of his existence was the enormous pile of burnt-out matches and broken biscuits outside the door of my little room every morning.

I used to wonder why they were always in the same place. Then very cautiously, the tramp made his appearance one day, and asked most deferentially if he could fill a plastic bottle with water. In the afternoon he reappeared with the same request, spoken in such a gentle, appealing upper-class accent as to sound almost melodious. His mild brown eyes expressed a humorous anxiety and he wore a thin black duffle coat. His beard was dark, long and bushy, and his only possessions at that time were a brown blanket and a leather bag for his biscuits.

One morning I came in and found the Commander slumped on the floor across my doorway, with the blanket over him and drawn over his head, and crumbs and matches all around. I thought my worst fears had been realised and that a tramp had died on me. Tremulously, I pulled back the blanket and the Commander smiled up at me agreeably.

'Good morning, my dear fellow!' he exclaimed. 'What time is it?'

I told him and he arose, stretched himself and went out for a walk. Apparently, my doorway was his sleeping place. After that we became good friends, and he told me that he wasn't a Commander at all, but merely a retired Lieutenant, and I must call him Jim.

'One of the strangest things I've ever seen,' he told me 'was an albino stoat. It must be very rare – a pure white stoat.'

'Was it an ermine in its winter coat?' I asked him.

'No, it had no black tip to its tail. It was a pure white stoat! Last winter when there was snow, I had a sleeping bag, and with permission I slept in the woods in the grounds of that big mansion that's now a girls' school. There was a glade in the wood, and there I lit a fire and sat up eating biscuits. All around, like little sparks, I could see the eyes of field mice in the undergrowth. Then if I lay still they would run out and dance around eating the crumbs. One night, I looked and along ran this *dear* little animal, a pure white stoat! It hunted the field mice, and soon they didn't come any more. Finally, the stoat began to eat crumbs itself. You won't credit this, but after several weeks it began to crawl into the bag with me when it thought I was asleep. My body kept it warm, you see, and it would curl up next to me. One night I woke up to hear a crunching noise and I thought what the devil's that? It was the stoat eating one of my biscuits, which it had dragged into the sleeping bag with me! Enough is enough! I got up and shook it out, and after that it never came again. What a lovely little animal!'

'Are you sure it wasn't a ferret?'

'No, it was too small and dainty. An albino stoat – an extra *ord*-inary rare animal.'

At first I assumed that Jim was a carefree tramp of romance, but before long he began to speak to me in distressed tones of voices that persecuted him by night, beamed onto him by the government. He thought there was a plot to murder him and he spoke continually of seeking political asylum in Russia. Another of his pet ideas, spoken of with real vehemence, was of the need to chop off the Queen's head. A *most* unseasonable thought for the Year of Jubilee.

Tom, my Liverpool friend, told me that Jim paced up and down every night, raving aloud and striking matches which he hurled to the ground. This considerably annoyed the other five tramps who slept in the newly-opened washroom. One morning, I found an awful mess, as Jim had unwittingly set fire to the full litter basket and then emptied water over it. He smoked a cosily smelly old pipe and so I suppose he needed matches.

Then Jim vanished and a trampish rumour had it that he had been sent to prison for hitting a policeman with a bottle. Finally, it turned out that he was in a mental home, and he soon reappeared, the same as ever, though 'under section'. Once a fortnight he had to report at the asylum, perhaps spend a night there, and then go back to the toilet and the voices. This was called 'returning the patient to the Community'.

'How are you today? Good, good, fine!' I could imagine the doctor saying blithely. 'Home circumstances okay? Good, good, fine! Do have a cup of tea while you're here.'

Meanwhile, back in the community of toilet-living madmen, Jim had a spot of luck. He was befriended by a young German on holiday, who bought him a rusksack, sleeping bag and spirit stove, and gave him a lift to Guildford. It was now the height of summer, and Jim spent a month sleeping in a field near Guildford, and then returned to the toilet with his treasures. He sold all but the sleeping bag, and a new phase of his life began.

Above the toilet was the park, and near the lavatory railings grew a dense shrubbery of dark bushes. Jim made a cave-like home inside a bush, and slept there in his sleeping bag. By day he kept his belongings there, including a deck chair which he had found somewhere. During wet weather he would take this chair down to the toilet and I would let him sleep in it in a corner of the washroom, to the surprise of customers. Finally an irate deckchairman took it back to the beach, and I gave Jim a spare chair from my room that I thought no one would miss. It was taken away as well, to Jim's chagrin, but he pinched a better one back again.

Unlike most of the other tramps, Jim always had enough to eat, as he had a small pension from the Navy. The corner·post office, a cheery little shop, was also a general store and the owner let Jim use it as an address, and also gave him tick between Fridays, deducting it from the pension when it came. Jim would sometimes come along with his bag full of biscuits, ginger cake and bottles of lemonade, and we would have feasts in the bush hidey-hole or in the toilet when wet. A generous man, he would share his all with the other tramps and the bush was often crowded. I didn't like to take too much, but who can resist ginger cake and lemonade when offered?

Sleeping out of doors seemed to waft away the voices and as the Welfare were said to be finding him a room, I felt I had every reason to be optimistic about Jim.

*

A genuinely carefree tramp, usually tipsy and with a ribald attitude to life, was Mr Templeton. For some reason, he was known by his surname, which suited him. Mr Templeton was a tall strong man in his sixties, with a light brown coat, a dark brown bag and white wavy receding hair. With his cloudy blue eyes, small hooked nose and long shaven chin, his face was marvellously expressive. Usually it expressed humour, but when it registered Annoyance, it was no less comic, because of its candour. Mr Templeton had been a tramp uninterruptedly since the Thirties, and took a keen interest in people and places.

I first became aware of Mr Templeton when the washroom at the Seafront was opened, cleaned and put into use. Next morning, I found that one of the basins was full of tea leaves, for the water was hot enough to brew up with. Soon I caught Mr Templeton in the act, mug to his lips and tea leaves everywhere. I hadn't realised he was a tramp before, although I'd seen him everywhere, and the small ticking off I gave him helped to break the ice. Tramps can be spoken to without the slight effort and pretence needed when talking to workmen, who tend to value a matter-of-fact and strictly commonsense outlook on life at the expense of abstract ideas. I found it relaxing to meet people who, like myself, did not understand cars or television, and so I welcomed the agreeable company of Mr Templeton.

A great one for conversation, Mr Templeton, punctuated his remarks with enthusiastic cries of 'looksy! looksy!', his way of pronouncing 'look, see'. As the level in his cider bottle fell lower and lower, the 'looksies' flew thicker and faster, his smile grew more and more fatuous, his head began to nod like a wooden pecking-chicken toy and his hands to shake as if he was fanning the air. Generally, at this stage, he would be agitated about something. Usually it was the vicar.

I knew this vicar, a Low churchman who had taken a High parish in a nearby village and put pillow cases over the figures of the Virgin. Himself every bit as comical as Mr Templeton, he had caused great scandal and offence by appearing suddenly, in mid-service, in the Baptist congregation. These good people met in a converted cowshed belonging to the parish council, and their first thought was that the vicar had come to size the place up before seizing it as a church hall. Probably they were right, but however worthy the Reverend's motives may have been, he showed the cloven hoof once and for all in Baptist eyes by *kneeling to pray*. He prayed long and fervently, with his eyes shut and everyone staring at him suspiciously; but to no avail, as when I last enquired, the Jehovah Witnesses were making the strongest bid for the cowshed.

At a slide show in the vicarage, which I attended, imported evangelical types mixed oddly with the good county stock who attended church. When the lights went on, an agitated tremor ran along the regular church goers, who looked like retired colonels and their wives, affable and good at running fêtes. Their leader seemed to be a tall hawk-nosed man, with a tanned crinkled face, alert bird-like eyes and a long faded military moustache with frayed ends like tobacco drooping from a roll-up. You expected him to peer from a raised visor, an old Norman veteran of the Crusades. He jumped to his feet with a brisk apology, and whooshed out of the door with all his retainers, just as the vicar announced Spontaneous Prayer as the Spirit Descends. This interruption gave the evangelicals time to think of their Spontaneous Prayers.

To cut a long story short, this vicar had a caravan in his garden, and he let Mr Templeton sleep in it. You would have thought that this was a happy ending, and that Mr Templeton would live there for ever afterwards, but far from it.

'That blasted vicar, looksy! He's driving me mad, I told him, looksy, looksy! Looksy, he talks all the blasted time! Last night I got in at midnight, looksy, and climbed into bed. Bang, bang on the window! Oh my Gawd, "looksy, who can that be?" I thought, looksy? It was the blasted vicar!

' "Can I come in for a chat?" he asks, looksy. At two o'clock in the bloody morning! "I can't sleep" he says, looksy.

' "Looksy!" I told him. "I need my bit of peace and quiet same as any man, looksy. Why don't you shove off?" I asked him, but he's already *in* and talking away fit to bust, loosky!

' "Looksy, blow that," I thought. 'I'll be off out of there tomorrow. I'm not going back there to that blasted vicar – he'll drive me mad, he will, looksy." '

'Aren't you a bit ungrateful, Mr Templeton?' I enquired.

'What for, that caravan? He knows what he can do with his caravan, looksy, I'm much happier on a bench – much happier. Everyone ought to sleep on benches! It's the only life!'

As he declaimed these possibly immortal words, Mr Templeton looked most idealistic. Workers of the world, unite – you have nothing to lose but your beds!

When crossing the town centre, I often saw Mr Templeton with his cider bottle on a bench in front of the bank.

'I don't need to worry, I've got money behind me!' he would say, chuckling and jerking a thumb back at the austere building.

One day to my surprise, he acquired a girlfriend. This was an old lady of eighty, with her hair in a bun and a blissful pop-eyed expression on her face as she sat on the bench holding hands with Mr Templeton. There, for the next few weeks, I was to see them every day. Whenever Mr Templeton got too saucy, she walloped him over the head with her walking stick, for she was full of spirit.

However, one day she ran up to me, almost in tears.

'Mr Templeton has gone away! she told me. Apparently for all their whispered endearments and shared 'looksies', he was still 'Mr Templeton' as ever. 'Where do you suppose he can be? One of his friends told me he was in prison. I do hope he's not suffering, for all that he made me suffer.'

'Oh dear! Come to think of it, I haven't seen him round the toilets for a few days. Whatever would he go to prison for?'

'I don't know, but he was a bad man, that Mr Templeton. I couldn't believe it at first, I thought he was such a gentleman! I've got a little council house and once I'd asked him in, you never heard the language he used! Terrible! And the things he called me! "You'll have to leave now, Mr Templeton," I said. But bad as he was, I'd hate anything to happen to him.'

It seemed that there was a darker side to Mr Templeton – he bit the hand that fed him. A few weeks later he returned, as blithe and chirpy as ever, although his romance was not taken up again. He had not been in prison at all, but had hitch-hiked into the West Country and back, staying at Plymouth and Exeter.

'I always go travelling', he said. 'Looksy, looksy, I was in Warrington once, and I sees a lorry. Up goes the old thumb.'

' "Where are you going to?" asks the driver.

' "Wherever you're going," I says.

'Turns out, looksy, he's going to Penzance and then back to Warrington. That suits me, I tells him, and I hops in and that night I'm in Penzance. Next morning, I waits at his lorry, looksy, and get taken back to the identical spot at Warrington. That's what I call travelling, looksy. Now see what I've got – a new blue spirit stove, that fits in my bag and all, looksy. Now I can heat tins, brew up and everything.'

Mr Templeton and Commander Williams (Jim) became friends, the former supplying heat and the latter food. With their tins of soup bubbling away, they were rather a nuisance to customers in the washroom and I had to keep shooing them into corners or out into Jim's bush if an inspection seemed imminent. But when the season was almost over, and I was to retire for that year, I let them have a full scale picnic in the lavatory, to which Liverpool Tom was invited. During the winter, the toilets went to rack and ruin anyway, being cleaned very quickly in the early morning by Ken or the Foreman, and then left to fate, tramps and Mombops.

Overjoyed with their new freedom, Mr Templeton and Jim grew busy, and as I left they were mashing potatoes in a wash basin and frying sausages over the flaring stove on a dustbin lid. A small boy stared at them incredulously.

'Looksy, hoppit sonny, or I'll give you one!' Mr Templeton threatened sternly.

Not all the vagrants made pleasant companions – some were very unpleasant, and made the cleaner's life most difficult. If you can cast your mind back to the beginning of this saga, you'll remember the occasion when a tousle-haired blond boy with a sleeping bag holed up in a toilet and only came out when I threatened to call the police. I directed him down to the Seafront toilet, as a place where he could lie in a bit longer. Bitterly did I regret this act, as he became the bugbear of the place.

To my annoyance, he jammed himself into cubicles with his sleeping bag, and later in the day proved very hard to dislodge. On one occasion he turned up with a brand new guitar and said a friend had lent it to him. That evening the guitar was gone and he had plenty of money to play the pin-tables in the local workman's café. Among his belongings, which I stored in a cupboard in all innocence, was a large torch. Slowly came the realisation that my young blue denimmed guest was a thief.

Also among his belongings, to my surprise, was a tattered copy of *Tess of the D'Urbervilles*.

'S'only a rubbish old book,' he responded to my cry of surprise.

'It's a very well-thought of book that', I told him reproachfully, wondering if he had hidden depths.

'Oh yeh, well I meantersay, it's really good, yeh,' he answered, so I concluded that he hadn't.

He'd probably pinched it, but the owner's loss was my gain. At last I was able to read it right to the end, up to where the President of the Immortals, or Hardy himself, has finished his sport with Tess.

Next morning, when I arrived at the Seafront, I found to my horror, that all the lights were on. Somebody was in my room, where the switches were. Hastily I burst in, quick as key could turn, and found it was the wretched youth in his sleeping bag. He had climbed over the wall, which did not meet the ceiling. Not only that, but he refused to get up, no matter how much I prodded him. I took his torch and burglary kit outside, but he was too heavy to lift.

'Sit up, I can't have you in here!' I wailed.

'No!'

'Look your arm's all running with blood!' I exclaimed truthfully. 'You must have cut it on the broken glass where the window's boarded up. You'd better get up and wash it!'

'Didn't cut it on no broken glass!' he replied decisively. I couldn't open the cupboard where the brush and pan were, with him lying there.

'Everything all right?' came a welcome voice from the doorway.

It was Ken, so I explained the situation. He kept calm and simply called Harry the Dustman who was parked nearby. Harry, muttering curses of loathing against all idle vagabonds, picked up an iron crank shaft handle and stomped down the steps. He was an enormous man. Ken and I waited at the top of the steps, and in a second or two the young man walked out in scornful deliberation, refusing to be hurried too obviously by the wrathful Harry. After that, he stayed in town for a day or two, but never bothered me again.

When I cleaned up after him, I found an empty syringe, so his arm may have bled after an injection of heroin. Before disappearing from town the young man came into the orbit of Mr Templeton, who didn't care for him.

'That young fellow, looksy, has jumped bail somewhere – he's on the run. Surly young bastard he is, too. Looksy, yesterday on the bench he was telling me to go ringing front doorbells asking for a glass of water, while he nips in the back and robs the places.

' "You're off your head!" I tells him, looksy. "Do you think I'm going to stand there like a muggins while you get away with the loot? Every copper for miles'd be after me," I told him, looksy. He didn't like that. Ah he's no good, not him, no good at all, looksy.'

'Mr Templeton, sir, you're an excellent judge of character,' I replied.

Two very unpleasant characters who took up a lot of my time were Sir John and Beaky. It was not just that they were raving mad, as we all have our eccentricities. They had each an air of violence about them, and an uncanny touch of the sexual offender. Sir John inhabited the Seafront, as a rule, and Beaky the Manor House. Later I introduced them, hoping that they would destroy one another, but no such luck. They became friends instead, and Sir John treated Beaky to enormous meals of baked beans.

I first became aware of Sir John by a loud raucous singing coming from a cubicle, which startled both the customers and myself. Several sentimental songs later, the voice changed to a loud swearing directed at the world in general. Finally I had to sweep and mop the compartment, so I knocked and entered. Sitting among empty barley wine bottles, reading a semi-legal picture magazine, was a glassy-eyed middle-aged man with a clipped military moustache and the look of a broken down salesman about him. He came out politely, holding a gleaming briefcase.

'Call me Sir John,' he exclaimed thickly, so I did.

No one else agreed to call him this, apparently, so he took to me at once, to my great annoyance. Every day he stood and talked and talked and talked, saying the same things over and over again.

'Yes, Sir John' and 'No, Sir John' I said wearily at intervals, moving him from place to place as I cleaned.

'I told you I was going to sue the council, didn't I, for letting me fall down the stairs? They don't know who they're tangling with! I'm a friend of the Chief Constable, you know. I'm a CID man, a CID man – they don't know who they're playing with! Not only that, but I've got the VC Look, I'll show you! [Here he would remove his tie pin, which was shaped like a sword.] See that – a VC for conspicuous gallantry. I'm a Gurkha, you know. I was a Gurkha in the war, a national hero. Look, here's a photo of my wife. A lovely woman – she won't have me back. I've got some photos of nude models here somewhere – look! I know her, I can fix you up. Yes, I'll show them – I'm a man of power! I've got my own business and ten men under me! Now I must go and see about my business.'

At last he would walk out, singing loudly. He always had pockets full of pound notes, and by his clothes, it looked as though he had been a commercial traveller who had suddenly gone mad and had never changed clothes or slept in a bed since. You could trace his progress about town by the empty barley wine bottles he left everywhere. Sir John's fat bogus-colonel features were comically expressive, whether he was in a smug mood, or power-crazed or in agitated pop-eyed anguish over something.

Quite often he would get into fights, suddenly shouting insults at tough-looking people, doubling his fists and shouting 'Come on! I've got a black belt in judo – scared, aren't you?'

Funnily enough if this warlike approach worked, and the tough or group of toughs attacked him, Sir John would suddenly change and run away in terror. If I was there, I could quickly calm matters by saying, 'It's all right, Sir John, this man's your friend; he's done you no harm.'

As soon as the insulted person realised from my tone that Sir John was mad, he would laugh heartily and go away. So I was used to seeing Sir John with a black eye or bruises, but the morning that he staggered wild-eyed into Manor House covered in soot was a startling occasion.

'The bastards blew me up with a bomb!' he shouted 'Now the manager's thrown me out! He said I was smoking in bed!'

This would be a good beginning for a novel and aroused my curiosity. Bit by bit the truth came out. Sir John, in the evenings, used to hang around a low drinking club in the docks, where roulette was played until the small hours. Perhaps he was better behaved there, and may have been useful emptying ashtrays or whatever, as the manager let him sleep in a shed in the back-yard on a pile of sacking. It was this shed and sacking that had caught fire as Sir John slept, and the manager had been furious. Sir John himself was none too pleased to wake up and find himself in a raging inferno, but he had escaped somehow. He persisted with his bomb theory, but as he was a heavy smoker, I secretly sided with the manager.

This episode made Sir John inferno-conscious, and for the next few weeks he wandered around with an empty paraffin can, saying that he was going to burn down the club and the council offices. If he had ever bought any paraffin, I might have gone to the police. He easily beat Jock to the title of Most Hated Man on the Road and indeed Jock told me, in a most scandalised voice, that Sir John hung around the convent girls' school and offered the pupils money at going-home time.

Every now and then, Sir John fancied he was a police officer, and from a pedestrian's point of view it was quite funny to see him directing traffic. He would stand in the middle of the road and roar at the top of his voice, waving his arms in frantic meaningless signals and swearing at the drivers, who looked terrified. In his heart of hearts, he must have known he wasn't a policeman, as whenever a real one came along, he would melt away. So much for Sir John. Now for Beaky.

Beaky was a young man with a fat face and a tramp's overcoat. He had black hair brushed forwards, a manner of self-important self-pity, and, in his more lucid moments, a merchant seaman's style of hardbitten conversation. I think he had been a seaman, but had taken to doing robberies while on leave, and had done time for stealing twelve hundred pounds from two Chinese brothers.

In the words of the local policeman, 'He's took so much drugs, he's done his brain in.'

I often had to consult this policeman about Beaky. Mr Virgo told me officially that Beaky was a hazard of the business, being violent, and I must get the police to move him on.

Emboldened by this advice, and annoyed at seeing Beaky take his trousers off in public, I told the miscreant, 'Out, you're barred!'

'You can't bar someone from a public lavatory,' he argued.

'You can be barred from a public house, so why not a public lavatory?' I countered.

To my disappointment, he went meekly, as I was looking forward to the excitement of a police attack – the Siege of Manor House. On other occasions when his meekness wore thin, I would cross the road and fetch the copper from the back of the greengrocer's. Breaking off in mid-flirtation with the assistant, the young bearded constable would quickly chase Beaky out and return to his dalliance among the Brussels sprouts. Then Beaky would wander off round the town, trying car door handles and lifting milk bottles from doorsteps in a desultory manner.

One day, so I heard, the old Cap'n had said to Beaky 'Hello old friend!'

'I'm not your bleedin' friend,' Beaky had replied, and attacked the Cap'n with blows to the face until dragged off.

For this he was locked up for a time and the whole town seemed to breathe a sigh of relief. That is the whole beauty of prisons – the benefit is not to the prisoner, of being reformed or rehabilitated, but to the public. Prisons give those outside a resting period from town bullies and horrible characters, and for this we should be very grateful. Beaky's conversation and behaviour was consistently revolting, and though he really belonged in a mental home, a prison was equally good from my point of view.

A few days later the Cap'n was back on the steps of The Crown, plus a few stitches in his face, animatedly drawing pictures for the crowd of children who clustered round him. He had great spirit for a man in his seventies.

I was lucky not to have more unpleasant characters on my rounds. Those who wrote perverted remarks on the walls came out in the evenings, when I was off-duty, and were gone by morning, as they lived in houses. Most of my daytime customers were kindly men who talked about the weather.

After a time, I found the cheapest transport café in town, and took extended lunch breaks to stroll over to it from the Seafront, making the time up afterwards. The café, a gloomy corner house among terraced streets, catered for busy and worthy workmen, with hot meals waiting dished out on red hot plates in the oven. A new road had been made nearby and a gigantic Continental-going lorry was often parked outside, for the husband drove while the wife served and cooked.

Curiously enough, a farm stood behind the café, surrounded by industrial scenery old and new. One side of the farm had been lopped off by the road and a new brick wall put up, but the rest of it had not changed much since the snug flint farmhouse was built. Obligingly, the builder had engraved the date on stone above the porch – 1770 A.D. Like a wrong piece in a jigsaw puzzle, with flowers around the door and a rooster and his wives scratching around in the straw-littered yard at the back, near the stables, the farm looked cosy and incongruous. No one I knew ever mentioned it, so perhaps it was invisible to most mortal eyes.

*

Naturally, in the Year of the Jubilee, every one of the terraced houses was gay with flags and pictures of Her Majesty. In some towns the jollity of the young people, particularly of teachers helping at celebrations, showed a curious mixture of patriotism, satire and camp humour, a legacy of the frightful Swinging Sixties. Union Jack chamberpots and the last night of the Proms evoke a similar mood. However, where I was, such sophistication was unknown, and the Jubilee was 'taken straight'.

There was a procession of drum majorettes, girls of twelve and thirteen, an ox roasted whole and other festivities, but down in the lavatories I saw nothing of these. People grew happy in the placid way of that half-asleep tea-drinking town, and an elderly nun from the convent school told me most fervently that the Royal Family set a wonderful example to the nation by worshipping, televised, in Westminster Abbey.

It pleased me to see Royalty fulfilling its purpose, but I must give a black mark to the Royal duchess who visited the town, near the Seafront toilet. The nuns had lined the road on either side with merry little girls in grey uniforms and white ankle socks, with flags to wave at the duchess.

When I emerged from the underworld to go and have my lunch, it was a beautiful summer's day, and anxious nuns and cheerful girls were everywhere. Royalty had obviously been forgiven for the Reformation, and the nuns seemed more eager to see the duchess than anyone. Police stopped the traffic, and only a few cars were allowed through, cheered loudly by the schoolchildren, who must have been thankful for a holiday. When the Duchess came, she swooshed through town in about half a second, gazing woodenly forwards and quite ignoring the excited nuns and cheering children.

But for me, sitting on the grass, among the throng, this scarcely seemed an anti-climax at all. I had been well rewarded by the spontaneous singing of the girls. Again and again they sang the playground game-song of the moment, hundreds of treble voices that will always remain my happiest memory of the Jubilee.

'On a mountain stands a maiden,
But her name I do not know,

All she wants is gold and silver
All she wants is a fine young man.'

Earlier that day, Ken had spoken in warm praise of the Royal family, saying 'They're doing a difficult job.' As always when this is said, he seemed aware of having uttered a paradox. In this Total Work State there is no appropriate language for discussing Royalty. Surely they are not doing a *job*, clocking in each morning and watching the clock each afternoon! They should not be here to work, just to *be*, glorious and splendid, in palaces of gold if possible, and dressed in every finery, including crowns. Their existence helps the imagination to soar into fairy-tale worlds not very different from Heaven, and it is particularly the hard-working and unsophisticated subjects who benefit. For myself, it is the oldness and strangeness of Royalty that appeals, their ascent from forgotten days of barbarism, usually leading their people upwards. For every missionary knows that first you convert the king and the kingdom will follow.

From the transport café, as I was saying before the Jubilee overtook me, I would walk through town, by the river where the rock and souvenir shops were, and then along the prom back to the Seafront. The High Street contained many Welfare offices of various kinds, council departments, the Jobcentre, the Treasury and so on, mostly housed above shops and in odd corners, as well as in the nearby Manor House and a vast newly opened complex that dwarfed the church. After some months I pigeonholed the people of the town into three varieties, lower, middle and upper, or Tramps, Roadsweepers and Office Wallahs. The first two were the most intelligent, and the last were the most conceited. But it was a gentle conceit, in that dreamy office world where jargon and tea cups clinked together, and where, whenever I visited it on some errand, I was always struck by the relaxed atmosphere.

Welfare workers, supposed to visit hapless 'clients' once a week, never did so but sat making up reports and reading magazines. Somewhere there was a Rabies Control Officer, a Noise Abatement Officer and a Pre-Delinquent Youth Worker. There was no rabies, and by closing the door, the second officer abated all noise to the level of his own gentle snores. A proud man, the Pre-Delinquent Youth Worker claimed credit for every crime that did not happen, and they were manifold. He earned his twenty thousand a year, in his view, for his gift for spotting youths who were not delinquent yet, but going to be, and then stopping them. However, his club was never open and like the Youth Theatre Workshop was rented out by private arrangement for the use of crèches and play groups. So the wheels of the Welfare State went sleepily round as usual, taking money from people· and giving half of it back in a roundabout way, the difference going to the middlemen I have described. Better that such men and women be lulled into a half-sleep that suits their wits, than to wake them up and turn them loose on Society.

Outside in the streets, among the people who couldn't learn jargon, things were livelier, but often nastier. One day I saw a group of vindictive young shrew-faced housewives all squeaking their hate at an indolent shaggy-haired youth they had surrounded with their prams.

'You told them you was knocking me off!' a bleach-haired teenage bride snarled, eyes blazing.

Round the corner I heard a Hell's Angel say to his mate, with the utmost relish, 'Old Jerry's in court today. You know what for? Rape! The minimum's a fifty quid fine.'

When I was a teenager, rapists were scorned as unmanly perverts who couldn't get women. None of us could get women either, but we had a better alternative than rape, called Telling Lies. Now, thanks to certain books and films, rapists are manly, so I hope Jerry had been telling lies too.

Decent shop assistants and older shoppers made up most of the town, and the sordid was really the exceptional. Near the river I would always pause to gaze at a garden, belonging to a row of cottages that seemed to grow out of a flint and brick warehouse. Long ago, close-packed doors and small windows must have been inserted into a mill, forge or some such useful building, and then a garden made, with palings that separated it into strips, full of lettuces and beans, lean-to sheds and tipsy greenhouses. Over one of the doors, in a little cage, sat a pretty little goldfinch, red, yellow and black, and always singing. In a land held under the dread sway of the Wild Birds Protection Act such a Victorian sight is rare, and the goldfinch always delighted me. Its owner, a tough-looking workman, scowled at me suspiciously from time to time, as if daring me to report it.

The end of this odd wedge of cottages was a slope of roof that reached the pavement, the slates loose and scratched upon by children and teenagers with messages to impart. Next door was a busy sawmill, for the docks were opposite with stacks of imported wood. As the electric saw made such a loud whine, the young workmen wore ear-covers. Little businesses, in old fashioned or corrugated iron work-shops proliferated here, and most were nautical. A tiny chapel, with stained glass, had become a factory. By the river, an old man sold fishing bait from a crazy wooden hut on stilts, that sloped into the water.

Near where the river joined the sea, a wooden raft was moored to the jetty, bobbing up and down on the tide. Sometimes a small fishing boat was tied in turn to the raft, and fish were sold from its cluttered decks. A big brown dirty man with a wild beard stood gutting dogfish, one after the other, and two young boys wrapped them up in paper and handed them to customers. Useless crabs were disposed of by being hurled violently, while half alive, at the jetty wall, and on one occasion a gurnard was served in the same way.

Things were more pleasant by the sand dunes on the other side of the estuary, which could be reached by ferry boat. These tub-like black and white boats, each operated by a hairy youth, were little more than coracles with an engine and rudder attached. You paid ten pence on reaching the shore safely, and could then admire the dilapidated and ingeniously patched up rows of home-made houseboats imbedded in the mud. However, while at work, I didn't dare go on too many excursions, but hurried back to the Seafront to swab the basins.

Sometimes, when I felt rich, I dined in a Chinese Restaurant. There were two of these in town, one hushed and elegant, the other rough and ready.

In the first one, the tall thin waiter, a bespectacled youth, came from Hong Kong. A sensitive lad, he was deeply affected by Elvis's death, and liked to talk to me about the singer.

'Now he'll be singing to Jesus,' he told me gravely.

In the rough restaurant, a fat coarse-looking Chinaman would come forward and bellow 'All roight?' at you – his version of the town's typical greeting.

When four talkative West Indian women on holiday came in and sat down, he asked them where they were from.

'London!' they all replied at once, a bit offended. West Indians are sure that they are English, and not immigrants at all, at least as far as they think the world should be concerned.

As well ask a gipsy if he's a gipsy as ask a West Indian where he's from. Later he'll tell you with pride.

While discussing the waiter's cheek in loud voices, one of the women had a bright idea.

'Let's ask *him* where *he's* from!' she said.

When he returned with the 'plawn clackers,' they did so.

'China!' he replied, not surprisingly.

'What part?' they pursued.

'South China – Red China!' he told them, grinning with pleasure.

Perhaps he was a refugee from the Cultural Revolution, though I would have thought he had nothing to fear.

'He's friendly!' exclaimed one of the women in surprise, and all three discussed him animatedly until he came back with four empty glasses they had asked for.

Then from their handbags, they each took out a rum bottle and a

Coca Cola bottle, poured them into their glasses and had a very merry lunch indeed.

One Sunday in the transport caff, a curly-headed young workman joked, 'Why aren't you all in church?' Such jokes were common, and seemed to leave a sense of unease, as if the workmen *were* feeling guilty for working on Sunday and not going to church.

However, there *is* no church for workmen, unless they are born Catholics or are prepared to become teetotallers and go to chapel, a rather drastic step.

Near Manor House toilet, in a white building with enormous Gothic windows and a cottage attached, the Quakers met every Sunday morning. I went once out of curiosity, and found, to my happiness, that the service was one of complete silence from beginning to end. The spirit seldom descended on the genteel congregation and when it did, it did so quietly. So to that soothing former schoolroom I would go every other Sunday and have a really refreshing sleep. What bliss! Piously, I would offer a prayer to St Euchytus, the first man to fall asleep during a Christian Sermon and be unofficially canonised by myself for the deed, and then I would slip into sweet oblivion.

'Life is like a well-cut lawn,' I thought I heard a Friend say on one occasion, but it may have been a dream.

After the non-service, I would be given a cup of coffee by some white-haired old Quaker with a quavery voice. The Quakers went in for more left-wing and African causes than even the Anglican church could supply, for, as one well-spoken old lady told me, 'It's marvellous – throughout our history we've always been at the forefront of every Cause.'

These good people made a wonderful change from tramps, but their secular approach to religion had brought the Serpent into their Eden. In other words, one of the members had a fierce-looking son, a rabid Trotskyite. This boy was fawned on for his idealism and youth, and before long he was selling militant newspapers inside God's house, papers filled with crude praise for strikers, revolutionaries and atheists, and hate for anyone else. Despite my own villainy of using the place as a dormitory, I was deeply shocked.

By mid-September, although the weather was at its hottest, by council ruling the Summer of 'Seventy-seven was at its end, and my job with it. With many invitations to return next year, I went round shaking hands and making my goodbyes. Ken the foreman, Laurence, Mr Templeton and Commander Williams had become good friends of mine and I promised to keep in touch.

One of my last customers at Manor House was a pigeon. A grounded wood pigeon, to be more precise. Its self-important waddling entrance amused the other patrons, some farm working types who told me to wring its neck and pop it into a pie. Instead I cornered it where the weighing machine used to be, splattering feathers over my nice clean floor, and took it to the Lodge house Gothic cottage, once the schoolmaster's home, where a kindly Quaker lady said she would care for it and take it to the vet.

Then I went back, swept up the feathers and rode a Southdown bus out of town, never to return until 1978.

Next year, I met Ken and asked him the news. The little witch-like wizened lady cleaner had spent Christmas in Holloway Prison for forging social security forms. She had enjoyed every minute of it there, she said, especially the party.

Commander Williams, old bearded Jim, was dead. He had been found frozen to death in a lavatory cubicle, for although the Welfare had found him a room in Portsmouth, he wouldn't stay in it. Now the staff at the mental home could record that he had been 'returned to the Community' for the last time.

Everyone else was well. But later I met the old lady who used to conk Mr Templeton over the head with her stick, and she was very upset. Some boys, she said, had poisoned Mr T's cider, so she had heard, and thus disposed of him. It seemed likely, as there had been a short craze for killing tramps after the film *Clockwork Orange* came out.

Walking away, my head bowed, I almost bumped into a very welcome sight. 'Mr Templeton, *sir*! I thought you were dead'.

'Oh no, no not me, looksy. I got myself a tent and spent the winter camping in the woods near Windsor Park, looksy. Oh yes, I think I will have a bun. Looksy, let me tell you the latest about that blasted vicar . . .'

[PART THREE]
Meadowvale Dell

In the year 1890, Hamilton Allebone, a shoe manufacturer of Northampton, decided to 'set himself up as a gentleman'. Through hard work Mr Allebone had risen to be master of several factories and now he felt he should rest on his laurels.

Builders and gardeners set to work and the stately home of Meadowvale Dell arose, amid sleepy countryside, exactly halfway between Northampton and London. It was a large red brick manor house, with the customary Greek temple doorway fitted on, leading to a medieval baronial hall. An imaginative heraldic crest stood above the large fireplace, depicting a boar rampant. So far so good, and generations of little Allebones were soon playing all over the place. The house survived the First World War, but during the Second it was used for the troops, and barracks were built on the lawns.

When Hamilton's heir returned, in the late Forties, he found that the soldiers had wantonly smashed so much of his childhood home that he could no longer bear to live there. So the house became the property of the Government and in due course reopened as Meadowvale Dell Rehabilitation Centre.

This is where I came in. Applying to the Jobcentre once more in 1978, I was offered not a lavatory but a chance to be Rehabilitated. The same bright young lady took my particulars, I had a medical test and soon was hurrying to the station on my way to Meadowvale Dell.

It was not the first time I had heard of the Dell. Years before, a Welfare Worker had called on me, perturbed by the fact that I had never done any work. Concerned neighbours had sent her along, no doubt hoping that I could be got rid of somehow.

'I write novels a great deal, but they're never published,' I had told the forceful dark-haired woman.

Dismissing my dreams with a wave of her hand, the Welfare Lady asked me why I didn't get Rehabilitated.

'You can learn silk-screen printing,' she had declared soothingly.

Imagining this to be the art of making beautiful Japanese screens with pictures of cranes on, such as my grandfather had once owned, I agreed readily. However, she made enquiries about me, and after reading my grandfather's will, dismissed me as being 'not part of the Welfare State'.

Now, interested in a wry sort of way as to what the Welfare State would make of me, I was to be given a second chance. Months and months of Pupworth had made me eager for a change, and seized by wanderlust, I signed every paper I was given. I had been curious about the Dell ever since I had first heard it described as a place where people who had been out of work for years could gently be eased back into harness over a two month course. I had never been Habilitated in the first place, and part of me yearned to be ordinary, and to fit my lack of exam results. These had graded me as 'working class'; wrongly, since I had no manual abilities. Dismissing this sentimental part of me as a hippie in quest of Oblivion, I vowed to take life as it came, expecting no miracles and bearing ill will to none. My curiosity deepening, I changed trains in London and sped on shiny rails to Meadowvale Dell.

'Bloimey, I were that *drunk* last ni-ght after five double vodkas!' a voice shouted. Looking up I saw a very cheerful, forceful young man with cropped hair and a broken nose. His face was red, his body small and somewhat twisted looking, and he wore enormous boots. It was not I that he was addressing in a jovial Norfolk-Cockney accent, but an old lady at the far end of the carriage. So jolly and devil-may-care was his manner that his listener was quite charmed, and smiled fondly at him as he launched into fantasies of alcoholic stupors as yet unknown this side of the Iron Curtain. Every time the train slowed down, his expression changed to one of acute anxiety.

'Is this the station for Meadowvale Dell?' he would ask.

After a while, the old lady got out and four very boisterous West Indian girls clattered into the carriage. Now our hero was in his element, and soon he was monopolising their equally noisy conversation. The whole carriage seemed to roar in merriment. All too soon, our fateful station was reached, and the young man wrenched himself away from four admiring glances and swaggered out onto the platform.

'Yes, I'm for the Dell, too,' he told me. 'Call me "Chips", that's what everyone calls me back in Norfolk where I comes from. This way, this wa-ay, there's supposed to be a van picking us up.'

Three other young people, dim, nervous and vague in comparison with Chips, stood behind the small red-brick station, staring uncertainly around. Within minutes we were informed that Chips's father was a tractor driver in a remote country village, that Chips himself was an expert poacher, handy with an airgun, and that he belonged to the Terriers, but suffered from a bone disease. All this seemed to be true, but as the van was rather late in arriving, he could not resist describing imaginary scenes of active service in Ulster, magnifying the Territorial Army into a crack regiment, the scourge of the IRA.

'You Rehabilitees?' another voice called, and we obediently climbed into the back of the van from Meadowvale Dell. Through the rear window, I could see the small market town vanishing below us, as the road unrolled its way through opulent parkland, chestnut trees towering over demesne walls. At the top of the hill, we swung into a rhododendron tunnel, past a gateway with a large yellow sign reading 'Government Rehabilitation Centre'.

Climbing out, I looked in dismay at an ugly brick annexe, with a concrete ramp for wheelchairs leading up to a door marked 'Reception'. Three tall oafish-looking young men jeered at our bewildered faces as we emerged from the van, dragging our heavy luggage.

'Suckers! You don't know what you let yourself in for!' they guffawed. Inside, in a dimly-lit corridor, we sat on waiting room chairs amid piles of bags and suitcases. Rehabilitees of every kind kept arriving, until we were fifty strong, if strong is the right word. Some hobbled on crutches, others were brain-damaged and could not speak or co-ordinate their movements, and some held up withered hands as if for a healing touch. Instead of a Saviour, we were confronted by an officious-looking man in spectacles, who introduced himself as Ron. Gathering around him, we awaited our introductory speech. The halt and lame were a minority, and I was not over-impressed by the old lags and persistent scivers, older men with brutal faces, full of beer and bitterness. By a natural process, I found my place in the Dell among the teenagers, twenty years my junior and more, who seemed far more fresh-faced and innocent than their more fortunate brethren in colleges and discos. Many were village boys from remote moorland, fenland or mountain parishes, who could find no work on the farms in which their fathers had laboured before them. Most of these lads eagerly hoped to be transformed into skilled mechanics and factory workers. Anyone who fears for the survival of England's rural accents need only visit Meadowvale Dell to be reassured.

One boy, to his shame, was brought by his mother. Soon to be known to us all as Geordie, he came from a remote corner of County Durham, and had stopped growing four years earlier when he was thirteen, and had crashed his motorbike during a rocky overland scramble. Geordie's dialect was hard to understand at first, but once his mother had left, his spirits rose to an almost Chips-like level. Words often used for Northerners, such as 'doughty' and 'plucky' sprang to mind on meeting him, and he and Chips were soon to become 'best mates'. Many of the brain-damaged, unable to speak or to move normally, yet with minds at work in terrible isolation, had been motorbike victims. They formed living reproaches to anyone foolish enough to yearn for the Romance of the North Circular Road, neon lights and racing with the devil on your side.

'I never 'phone my Mum at night,' a crippled youth told me, later on. 'My older brother's got a motorbike too, and she has a fit every time the 'phone goes, thinking that he's been in an accident as well.'

Girl and boy Rehabilitees stared at one another hungrily or questioningly. Romance, engagements made and broken within hours, proved to be the stuff of which Government Rehabilitation was made. One young lady with a tragic, sensitive face of great beauty, looked up from her wheelchair with large brown eyes. She snorted in derision as Ron made his speech and then handed out lapel stickers with our personal numbers on. These last were mildly protested against, but only because they kept falling off. After a week, nobody wore them any more, as by then we had memorised our numbers.

'Nah then, you lot,' Ron said with attempted bluffness. 'I'm giving you the keys to your rooms, and don't lose them. I don't want to hear anyone say "I've lost my key, Ron, let me in." '

For some reason, the supposed key-loser, as quoted by Ron, spoke in an idiotic nasal falsetto. Some of us tittered uneasily.

'He's trying to be one of the boys,' the wheelchair girl, Diana, told me. 'I despise that type. Authority should have dignity.'

We had to fill in a simple form, and Ron asked me if I could read and write.

'Yes,' I said cautiously.

'If you can't, we can give you lessons,' he explained.

Diana was among those who put up their hands to ask for help with the form.

'It says here "Home Address", but it doesn't say *which* home,' she said clearly. 'Should I put my town address or that of my country house?'

Everyone looked at her with interest.

'Some people have all the luck!' Ron, the supervisor, remarked, looking down at her wheelchair with scorn. 'The town house will do nicely, Your Ladyship.'

'You're not a Lady, are you?' I whispered.

'Of course not, I'm middle-class,' she answered, not deigning to look at Ron. 'Daddy owns Metalpart factories, and at weekends I stay in the lodge house at his country place near Buckingham.'

'Now take your belongings to your quarters, then come back here for the evening meal,' Ron commanded. 'You can use the reading room or art room, but don't forget! All sleeping quarters are locked up at ten at night! I don't want anyone coming to me moaning, "I'm locked out, Ron, what'll I do?" And in the morning, you're to be up at six, prompt for breakfast, medical examination, gym, and the training workshop. Oh yes, and always practice safety at all times. Safety is the coming thing in industry.'

Rows of long, low buildings, the Army barracks, left over from the war, stood to one side of the Big House. These were our quarters, cramped but comfortable, since the once-open dormitories had been redesigned as rows and rows of individual rooms, doors with windows in, and a long narrow corridor between them. Hot water rooms with boilers where clothes could be dried amid rows of steaming pipes, stretching in all directions, ensured that we were warm and snug. My room, identical to all the others, contained a bed, dresser and wardrobe, and a small window opening onto the lawns and chestnut trees outside. I unpacked and hurried back for dinner.

There was a long queue, and as I neared the counter at last, an old lag type, a big strong man, calmly pushed me back and stepped in front of me. I said not a word, accepting that Might was Right. Might could even be called the Basic Human Right, or a Natural Right. Civilisation could then be seen as the smashing of Rights and the granting of privileges. The food was excellent, and as I enjoyed my meal, who should join me but Chips, with his arm round a girl. To my amazement the girl was Cathy, the village 'bad girl' from Pupworth.

'Oh, hullo!' she said, without much interest.

An impish, short-haired girl, Cathy was slightly simple and very promiscuous, a burden to her genteel parents, who ran a wool shop. Chips was just getting into his stride, boasting of the Borstal he had done for G. B. H., when the tough who had taken my place in the queue jerked his head at Cathy, who followed him meekly outside. Chips recovered his aplomb in a moment, and began a long story about a ferret he had known in Norfolk. Cathy left shortly after I arrived, and there were rumours that the tough had been expelled on her account. With his departure, life at the Dell became more peaceful.

Older, unshaven men sat in the newspaper room in rows, each at a battered wooden desk. After reading a few papers, I went to bed. At ten o'clock the supervisor looked through my window to make sure I was in, checked every room in the row, and then locked the doors at each end of the barracks. It was my first night in Meadowvale Dell, and I slept soundly. All too soon the supervisor's knock aroused me for breakfast and my first working day as a Rehabilitee.

Everybody in the 'new intake' had to report to a prefab-like workshop where our 'basic skills' were to be 'assessed'. A gruff, kindly overseer asked us to stand in rows. Chunks of pink plastic were issued to us, along with various hacking devices. Our task was to chip the plastic into the shape of a paperknife and then shave it down into a neat semi-transparent blade. Puffing on a pipe, the supervisor strolled up and down the rows, offering a word of encouragement here and a stifled cry of dismay there. We were to spend a week at this task, and when we left the Dell, he told us, we could buy our own handiwork and take it home for an heirloom forever. Somehow I didn't think I'd bother.

Throughout my stay at Meadowvale Dell, I did not meet a single supervisor or welfare officer who did not address us as if we were children. It seemed the appropriate way to behave. Rehabilitees in their teens and twenties, as well as myself, responded to this treatment very well, frisking about, delighted with a word of praise yet not too dismayed by a frown, as somehow the Dell wasn't *real*. It wasn't school and it wasn't work, and if you couldn't do a certain task it didn't really matter. Those in authority really had no authority at all, and seemed to know it very well. If we were given useless jobs, so were the supervisors. The latter were in a worse position than were we Rehabilitees, as they were loaded with paperwork and directives from H. M. Government. In order to keep their shadowy employment, they somehow had to convince the high-ups at Whitehall or wherever that everything *was* real, with dynamic Rehabilitation going on right and left, in tune with the New Technology.

Meanwhile, as the week went by, I hacked cheerfully at my piece of plastic and made friends with others in my 'intake'. This was almost a fulfillment of an old daydream of mine – being allowed to have my schooldays over again without the worries, knowing in advance that exams didn't really matter and that even if they did, I couldn't pass them. Taking exams as seriously as my teachers had done had poisoned my adolescence. Yet when I left school, I found that no editor or publisher could care less if a writer had any 'O' levels or not, let alone higher qualifications. To my surprise, I found that many eminent men and women still alive had left school early and found their true vocations without a thought for tests and marks and mock 'O' levels. Much of my childhood had been wasted, but by a happy stroke of fortune I could now have it again at Meadowvale Dell. I looked around at my fellow-pupils.

All seemed fairly content except for the oldest among us, a big red-faced Yorkshireman with enormous hands and silver hair. He was in his late fifties, and could have been John Bull. While the youngsters prattled of this and that, and flicked bits of plastic at one another, the Yorkshireman looked back on his years of working life, now ended by factory redundancies.

'It's come to this, doing useless work with kids,' he told me. 'Yon supervisor *knows* all this is nonsense, I can tell.'

With a shorter lifetime of nonsense and uselessness behind me, I tried to put myself in his place, as someone shamed to have been on the dole instead of delighted to have received an allowance of free money. After seeking for work for two years, he had volunteered for the Dell in a fit of despair.

'Still, the youngsters here seem a nice lot,' I comforted him.

'They are that, a good bunch of lads. That's what makes me feel sometimes that there's no justice. Why should decent-living lads like these be hurt by motorbikes and crippled for life when Hell's Angels who terrorise neighbourhoods get off scot free? There *is* no justice!' and he hammered the workbench with his fist, making the plastic shavings jump.

His expression of honest wrath showed a conviction that Justice *ought* to exist, on earth as it is in Heaven.

Meanwhile, as the supervisor was on the 'phone, the young men, lame and sound, gathered around the beautiful wheelchair girl with two houses.

'Oh *Chips!*' she cried delightedly at a sally from that sprightly daredevil. As I approached, she looked up at me poignantly.

'Can you lift me out of my chair and help me to walk for a few steps?' she asked. 'I've been in this chair since I was knocked down by a car when I was fifteen, and I'm eighteen now. My doctor tells me that I should practice walking a few steps every day.'

I stood behind her and lifted her awkwardly to a standing position. She stood panting and I didn't dare to let go. All the boys, including Chips, looked at me expecting that I would make a semi-bawdy remark, such as 'Well, this is a bit of all right, isn't it?'

Instead, I kept a completely grave expression on my face, and so they too looked solemn and stared at the ground. Slightly releasing my grip, I allowed her to totter for three steps, whereupon she gave a gasp and seized the edge of the workbench for support. Chips and I slid the wheelchair back under her and she was sitting up examining the piece of plastic when the supervisor returned.

'I did walk, didn't I?' she asked. A chorus of voices reassured her.

'I found out about this place on my own, and decided I must do something for myself and try and find a way to be useful despite my accident,' she explained.

'Aye!' 'Yurr!' 'Roight!' a collection of country accents replied with approval.

Diana seemed very much at ease wherever she went, a remarkably unaffected girl, saved by her accident from the corrupting influences of university, 'debbing' and working for a glossy magazine.

Another girl with a great deal of spirit, who was busily trying to annexe Chips before the jealous gaze of other females, was Mandy. She was a tiny, tubby girl in jeans, with long auburn hair, thick lips that hung open and large eyes with a perpetual expression of humorous anxiety. Apparently she had been too wild for her parents to control, up in Cumberland, and a spot of Dell discipline was thought to be the answer. Mandy was always falling in love, and over in the girls' barracks, she kept her friends awake for hours while she talked about boyfriend troubles in a rapid Northern accent. Apparently, the girls shared rooms, to their evident enjoyment.

A young man I grew very friendly with, during our time spent whittling pink plastic, was Concorde. He didn't like this name much, but Concorde he was, for his nose was large and beaky, and resembled the famous aeroplane. However our Concorde's expression was jolly and boyish, quite unlike that of the nasty gnat-faced plane. He was a gangling sandy-haired boy of twenty, playful yet very eager to be good, and rather like a child of ten in many ways. A great one for playful punches and clumsy chases, Concorde could easily be reduced to tears by a bully. This very seldom happened, for he was well liked. With dogged determination, he struggled with his lump of plastic, constantly asking the supervisor for advice.

'At home in Yorkshire, I take the plate round in church,' he told me proudly. 'The Vicar always has a kind word for me. "Thee's a good lad," he said to me once. You'd like our church, it's a very old one.'

Nearly everyone I met here had a good word for God, and few doubted His existence. A cynical agnostic could make a case for his views by pointing out that the more half-witted the Rehabilitee, the greater the belief in God. The concept of a holy fool is an old one, and I prefer to think that emotions and instincts are a greater link with God than the intellect. Maimed, crippled and speechless, Rehabilitees often prayed to be released from their afflictions. During my time at the Dell, their prayers were not answered, but their faith remained and saved them from bitterness.

'If God wanted to cure me, He would,' said Dave, a married Welshman with sidewhiskers, reduced to crutches by the now familiar motorbike accident. This was said in great sorrow, not anger, and Diana comforted him.

A less pleasant youth was Arthur, a dark-haired boy, rather dandyish, who seemed to look on me with suspicion. He talked a great deal about girls, mostly to a thin freckle-faced boy from Berkshire called Nicky. An epileptic, with a silver medallion round his neck to prove it, Nicky was a comic, guileless lad, whose father was a village policeman. Most of the Dell epileptics wore medallions with an engraved message to passers-by who might come across them in a fit.

'I want to be a scaffolder when I leave here,' Nicky told me. 'That's a real man's job! I'll be up those high buildings like a fly, you'll see. Then after, with my wages, I won't arf drink a lot of beer! I'll be as stoned as a rat! Pint after pint, I'll drink.'

'I've drunk more than that!' broke in Chips.

'Have you ever had a girl friend?' enquired a squinting boy nick-named Dippy Ian. 'I'd love to get married and see what sex is like.'

Chips laughed at this, but Nicky had never considered the prospect of a love affair outside marriage, and he and Ian discussed their chances of matrimony.

'What's it like being married?' Ian asked Dave the Welshman, who was usually pining for his wife. Dave turned away without speaking.

'Every marriage is different, as every girl is different,' I tried to explain, the blind leading the blind. This idea was too much for Ian, who retired to his workbench.

One girl who was different was Lula, a dark-haired Greek girl, who walked with a painful limp. Her hair was long, her cheeks pink and her soul belonged to Jesus. In other words, she and her mother had been 'saved' at an evangelical church, and refused to attend Orthodox services, to her father's rage. Her home life in the Greek tailoring belt of Crouch End, North London, was rather stormy on this account. However, evangelical 'Youth Christianity', with its social life of folk-song and front room Bible readings, had given her an escape route from the usual strict confines of a Greek home. Already she was looking round for a church to go to.

The only boy in the workroom whose plastic paper-knife seemed more shapeless than mine was Dennis, a clerk-like lad with an expression of great pathos and solemnity, coupled with a fervent eagerness to please. Unfortunately, he could speak only in a whisper. As he tried to make himself heard, his right hand would rise towards his head and hang stiffly in a palsied position.

'Speak up! What's that?' Dippy Ian and Nicky would ask him at first.

Everyone else was scandalised at such tactlessness, and grew even more so when Nicky told Dennis that he ought to practise shouting, and he, Nicky would show him how it was done.

'Less noise there!' barked the supervisor a moment later, and we hurried back to our places. Dennis seemed very offended, but I cheered him up, and noted that his whispered conversations showed him to be far from simple. It was hard to see what the Dell could do for him, or anyone else for that matter. Where it failed in Industrial Rehabilitation, its avowed aim, Meadowvale Dale succeeded in creating a cheerful social atmosphere, where young people who had previously led isolated lives through misfortune could meet one another and play, flirt or gossip. If only the Powers that ran the Dell could realise this, they could refrain from persecuting the supervisors with demands for results and statistics. On the other hand, they might then decide to sack half of them.

On our first day we were all required to do Intelligence Tests, and Chips grew very excited. He felt badly about having no exam passes to his name. Now he could score a high IQ and redeem his opinion of himself! Unfortunately, we were not told the results of the test, but at least everyone could now imagine that they were top.

'I'm roight thi-ick, I am,' Chips said to me afterwards, however. Brightening, he went on to ask me all about Teddy Boys, imagining that all men approaching forty had been Teds.

I knew little of Teds, but our IQ tests had intrigued me. They had been printed during the war to test the brains of the troops, and the drawings of men entering mazes and so on always showed them in battledress with tin helmets on. On such ridiculous grounds as those quizzes the fates of thousands of lives might once have depended. Able men were no doubt barred from leadership and incompetents promoted. Returning to the present day, I confess I have no idea how I fared in the Intelligence Tests. Perhaps in fifty years time the figures will be released.

When the bell rang for gym, I was very apprehensive, for I had managed to be excused from this lesson at school, bearing the brunt of the ex-sergeant major's sarcasm with fortitude, as long as I didn't have to do terrifying things with bars, balls and vaulting horses. Now I had nobody to write a note for me. To my relief and delight we had a gym *mistress*, a jolly no-nonsense sportswoman in glasses, who cycled through the parklands with her old college scarf trailing in the breeze.

'Pull out mats, everyone!' she commanded.

All we were required to do was lie on mats bicycling our legs in the air or doing press-ups. The Yorkshireman was excused, and so was a stout sleepy-eyed old Liverpudlian, who told me he had once been a street singer. His Lancashire-Irish cynicism and amusement at life formed a pleasant contrast to the artless naivety of the youngsters. When it came to ball games, I managed to get excused all over again, and joined Yorkshire and Liverpool on the bench.

And so the first week at Meadowvale Dell flowed smoothly by, and at the end of it I had a very weird and wonderful paper knife to show for my pains. The only upsetting incident concerned Chip's mother, back in Norfolk. Somehow she had dropped a carving knife on her wrist, and found herself in hospital, fighting for her life. Chips was distraught, and ran around the place shouting the news to anyone who would listen. Many were the prayers sent up to Heaven on Mrs Chips's behalf for two tense days and nights. Then came the glad news that she had recovered and was on the mend.

'You gave us all a real froight, you know that?' I overheard Chips shouting at her on the 'phone. He would never talk if he could shout. Putting the 'phone down, he regaled me with a long account of a fight he had once with three Teddy Boys. The crisis was over.

Next day he was in a fright again, because he had lost Dippy Ian on a fishing expedition. Our weekends were free, but few of us went home. Some took a bus into the nearby town, some played in the gym and Chips and Dippy Ian had gone fishing.

'Why worry about Dippy Ian? He'll be all right,' I said.

'He's my mate, though, isn't he?'

83

Just then Dippy Ian blithely strolled up to us, soaked below his knees.

'There's a new bloke here with one leg half an inch shorter than the other. And the other is half an inch longer,' he observed mildly.

As the days went by, I grew quite accustomed to early rising. It was late September, and I would stand gazing out over the parkland of Meadowvale Dell from a little-used doorway halfway along the strip of barracks we lived in. A large welcome mat had been left outside the step for so long that green moss and blades of grass grew from it, and worms tunnelled through its entrails. Standing on this squelchy mat, I would gaze over the misty dew-damp meadows to the woods on the horizon. Here and there, in landscaped harmony, a chestnut tree stood with rufous or yellow stains spreading across its plume-like leaves. From amidst the far-off trees, a strange clock tower, with a golden dome and a weather cock, shone in the morning sun. This belonged to a college founded by a local benefactor who was said to have made his money from a cure-all quack medicine, 'Aqua Pompada'. Inspired by a French Chateau, Pompada Towers seemed so beautiful and extraordinary a building as to excuse any amount of misdeeds by its founder.

Once I had walked inside, posing as a mature student. Dusk, especially if swifts or swallows wheeled, always made me yearn for a golden age. Admiring the great fountain in the courtyard, I wondered that such a treasure could have been created less than a hundred years before, in 1883. In such a short time, the English have managed to lose a whole mountain range of talents. Beneath paintings of ancient worthies, I feasted on baked apple and syrup in the oak-panelled dining hall, suspected of being a non-student as I didn't know where the custard was.

Normally, however, I made do with the plain fare of the Dell, and then hurried to my morning tasks. Plastic paper-knives a thing of the past, we were now set to work in the garden. Diana and Lula had been sent to do office work and Chips and Geordie, to their great delight, were in the machine shop with masks and welding irons. The rest of our 'intake' would dawdle along beneath a beech avenue towards the kitchen garden. This lay beneath a bank on our right, with steps leading down to mellow red-tiled buildings, rows of greenhouses, and lettuce beds and marrow frames beneath a lichened wall. Beyond the wall stood the Edwardian cottages of local country folk, perhaps descendants of the first estate workers. A rather coarse lot, they resented the intrusion of crippled youths next door. Once I wandered outside the back gate and admired the cottage gardens, until a red faced rustic appeared and angrily asked me what I was doing.

'I'm from over the wall,' I replied, jerking a thumb.

To my surprise, this answer, which evidently explained all, reduced him to fits of convulsive laughter. Doubled up, he staggered into the house, bellowing, 'Over the wall, hoo hoo hoo!' and no doubt frightening his family.

Before starting work, we waited, sitting on a table and swinging our feet, in the changing hall where our boots, gloves and tools were kept. This hall had begun life as a chapel, and had then become a dairy, with a Gothic design outside and cool tiles on the walls within. Boys larked about and the fat old Liverpool busker cracked jokes. The few girls on garden work compared notes on whom they were engaged to at the moment. Most young Dell-dwellers emerged from their seven-week spell with five or more broken 'engagements' behind them, and emotional scenes were common.

Sometimes I had to fill large long-spouted watering cans from a duckweed-laden tank and water the plants. Hosing down the red brick paths was better fun, as I could then send spouts over the wall in hope of soaking the cottagers. Normally, however, my occupation was dismembering and replanting geraniums. We seemed to spend hours of our lives at this monotonous task. First of all you would cut off the shoots sprouting from a geranium stem and then individually pot each one. By a miracle of Nature, each shoot would become a geranium in its own right. It was rather like creating new life by cutting worms in half. Filling a pot with earth, we would add an inch of sand, and then take a special geranium-stick and poke a hole in this. The end of this mystifying process was when you stuck a geranium sprig in the hole and smoothed down the edges. And so the long day would wear on. The tedium for me was made bearable by the pleasant surroundings amid rare flowers and plants with purple pink-veined leaves. Our garden supervisor kept most of us well away from any plant more delicate than a geranium. Customers from the outside world drove up on occasion and bought flowers or seedlings, for Meadowvale Dell's policy was to try and be as 'real' as it could, with as much cause and effect and economic incentive as possible.

'All the supervisors are on rackets,' was how the Liverpudlian interpreted this, and he may have been right. Most of that harassed crew deserved their 'perks'.

Nicky, the young freckled epileptic, soon discovered the guardian spirit of the largest greenhouse, Edward the Toad. A large dark-skinned warty amphibian with belligerent amber eyes, Edward devoured the insect pests that lived beneath the pot-laden tables. Well-versed in the habits of toads, I caught a large worm and placed it beside Edward. An enthusiastic ring of Rehabilitees formed around the contestants, as the worm baiting began. Each time it was the same. Edward would squat with swelling throat and heaving sides, for he was a heavy breather, and the worm would seek for shelter under his tummy or webbed feet. Shifting awkwardly at first, like an absent-minded shopper in a crowd, the toad would suddenly realise what was what. With enormous concentration, his head would jerk down to face the worm, an expression of intense greed in his jewelled eyes. Wham! Down would go his head, and then up would go his hands to his mouth to push twirling worm ends back in like a clumsy man eating spaghetti.

Nicky and a boy called Stan grew touchingly fond of Edward. Sometimes they would give him a swim in the water tank, and then help him out again. I don't think Edward enjoyed his dips much, but he swam furiously, kicking out with his powerful back legs.

Stan was a jovial limping motorbike boy, with a round face and wiry National Health spectacles. He had come to grief, it appeared, through his liking for 'electric mild'; or beer with LSD tablets added. Motorbike races along hallucinating roads of glowing colours and changing shapes had been a short-lived fashion among his gang, who were no doubt short-lived enough themselves, carrying on like that. Funny names for drinks were Stan's speciality, and he constantly referred to 'mickey mouse' and 'lunatic soup'. He was going out with a rather simple, very respectable girl from the nearby town, a day attender at the Dell.

Arthur, the sneering well-dressed youth, behaved strangely in the greenhouses. Once I found him holding court before Nicky and company, as he tried to mesmerise a couple of blasé flower pots.

'By concentration and will-power, I can make objects move by themselves,' he explained, frowning severely. 'Soon those flower pots will begin to levitate.'

After several minutes, the flower pots remained where they were, but Arthur swore that he had seen them move. Irritated, the supervisor shooed us back to our tasks.

A few days later, Arthur was sent back to the institution he had come from. Apparently, he had greatly upset Lula and some other girls by trying to will them into falling in love with him. It appeared that his belief in mind over matter, a hangover of the Superstitious Sixties, had in some way sprained his brain.

'You should leave the devil alone – two of my mates went mad after seances,' someone remarked.

Lovers of 'lunatic soup' (Guinness) and other beverages could find a great deal to interest them in the Meadowvale pub, nicknamed 'Smokey Joe's' after its bearded landlord. A high gabled witch's house of a building, hung with fairy lights, it nestled among the edge of the dense woods that faced the gate to the kitchen garden, outside the grounds. Every night, to Smokey Joe's annoyance, both bars would be crowded with Rehabilitees. However, everyone had to be in at ten, the hour the locals rolled up to see the striptease.

'Tit show tonight,' Joe would tell them with sour satisfaction.

Rumour had it that the stripper was a coloured girl who dashed on and off the stage in five minutes on her way to a string of other engagements. Nicky fell madly in love with the Smokey Joe barmaid, a sweet red haired girl called Janice, who seemed very young.

Made a confidant as usual, I had to listen to Nicky's Bingo Little-like prattle of Janice and then carry love notes to her. Taking great trouble, Nicky drew a large heart with an arrow in it and drops of blood coming out. 'Nicky 4 Janice', he wrote on this, in quavery writing.

When Smokey Joe was at the back somewhere, I gave Janice the note and asked her if she wanted to meet Nicky.

'No, I can't.'

'Well, he's only a boy of course . . .'

'It's not that. I think he's handsome and I'd *like* to go out with him. But my boss won't let me go out with any of the Dell people.' And she threw a terrified glance at Joe over her shoulder.

Although the supervisors spoke to all Dell men as though we were children, they also assumed that our sole interests were drinking, gambling and women. Coy or not-so-coy references were made to the pub by any supervisors who sought to be 'one of the boys'.

The gardening supervisor soon grew tired of my clumsy efforts among the flowerpots, and he teamed me with Dennis the whispering clerk and sent us out with witch's besoms to sweep up leaves in the park around the Big House. I enjoyed this, for not only was the work soothing, but Dennis made a soothing companion. Unable to reply, he seemed to enjoy my monologue of chatter, and didn't flinch unduly when I burst into song. There was much to sing about, for despite barracks, buildings and buffetings of fate, the Meadowvale gardens remained as delightful as on the day of their completion. A formal sunken rose garden led through yew mazes to an arbour by a leaf-clogged pool. Most of the time we swept yellow leaves into heaps on the bright green grass between an avenue of tall poplars leading to the mansion's front door. Sometimes I would stand portentously on the front steps of the house, trying to imagine myself as a country squire and owner of all I saw. I succeeded only in feeling like Toad of Toad Hall, and in fact I caught a real toad near the steps and put it in the greenhouse with Edward. But it was never seen again.

In a quiet corner of the grounds, in a little gazebo, stood a white statue of a flimsily draped woman holding a baby. One of her arms had been broken off, and her eyes were sightless in the classical tradition, but I was enchanted by her. Perhaps she was a goddess. At all events, I would steal away to worship the spirit of sweet, innocent, absurd Victoriana, before such monstrosities as world wars, prefabs, strip shows and jargon about Rehabilitees had been invented.

Racking his brains to think of a job for Dennis and myself, the supervisor led us to a compost heap in a shady glade.

'Look, whenever Rehabilitees wheel compost up to this tip they have to cross this bumpy piece of ground and half the stuff falls out,' he said. 'See all these bits of paving stone? Dig shallow squares out of the earth and press those slabs into them to form a path for the wheelbarrows, like a crazy paving. Fill in the gaps at the edges with earth and smooth it all down as flat as possible.'

The slabs were very heavy, and the job took us a week. As we worked, I rhapsodised eloquently over the splendour of our task, comparing it to building the Taj Mahal. At last it was finished.

'For centuries our work will stand!' I cried, to a burst of imaginary background music, that, helped by an equally imaginary angelic choir, rose to a crescendo as I spoke. 'Rehabilitees yet unborn will wheel their compost smoothly to the tip without spilling a drop and bless the unknown men who made that path. Visitors to Meadowvale will be shown that path as the highlight of their tour, a triumph of Man's struggle against the inexorable forces of Nature. We have created something as permanent as Man can hope to make in these uncertain times when civilisations collapse and Empires topple. One day Meadowvale Dell may be no more, its supervisors forgotten, yet *that path* shall still remain as ever, guiding the curious traveller to the very rim of the compost heap . . .'

I could have continued at some length, but glancing up I noticed that Dennis's eyes were fixed on me in a glow of admiration. He was deeply moved, and had taken my remarks quite seriously. Henceforward, whenever he met me he would take a deep breath, raise his right wrist and whisper, 'I saw the path today. It still seems to be all right.'

To my regret, the gardening course came to an end, and we were to be sent on to the workshops to do Light Industry. Most of the boys were delighted at this, as even the most skilful geranium potters had no desire to take up a career in gardening. However, an older Rehabilitee, an ex-hippie with a bad leg (motorbike) had been a farm labourer before his accident, and hoped now to take up market gardening. An intelligent man, only very slightly LSD-addled, he had been to art school years before, and had slipped easily into tractor-driving for an eccentric squire, while recuperating from the late nineteen sixties. He had married a country girl, and lived with his wife and children in a tied cottage.

'My employer won't turn me out until I've found another job,' he assured me. 'He's a nice old boy, and he seems to take me for a nineteenth-century villager. For years he paid me twenty-eight pounds a week, and when I asked for more he said he couldn't afford it, but he'd let me shoot rabbits and collect firewood in his woods. So we lived on rabbits for ages, and then just before my accident last year he raised my pay to thirty six pounds a week. I don't know what we'll do now. Farm labourers live in another world to the working man. A bloke I know worked for a small farmer, and he left the field in the middle of hay-making 'cos his wife was in labour over in the cottage. That farmer was furious! He docked the bloke his wages and would have sacked him, only he couldn't have got anyone else. I'd hate to work indoors for a living now, all the same, even though my wife'd welcome a change from skinning rabbits.'

With my entry to the world of Light Industry, a grimmer atmosphere seemed to take over Meadowvale Dell. Together with the sturdier youth bound for the machine shop, we had to hurry to work in the morning and punch a time clock in the wall. Chips, Geordie and others seemed ecstatically happy playing with dangerous looking machines. Fitted out in a blue denim worksuit perhaps made for a child, Geordie was in his element, clinking about with a spanner in his hand, looking purposeful and fulfilled. Us lesser lights had to cross the iron-shaving spattered floor of this man's world in order to reach the Cuckoo Shop, as our long room with rows of benches was termed. Our supervisor was Mr Petherington, a balding man with glasses. Despite his brown overalls, he looked like a thwarted income tax clerk. We were doing 'real work', assembling goods for actual firms who had made a bargain with the Government. In some official mind, or scheme, or file, we were part and parcel with Borstal Boys and convicts who also did 'real work' on Government contract.

On the wall hung an achievement chart covered in zig-zag lines, and Mr Petherington forever had his eye on this, for on it his prestige and perhaps his wages depended. There was a works office nearby, where both machine and Cuckoo Shop workers had to queue every Friday for our weekly twenty pounds.

'How are you adjusting to your wage?' the social worker lady asked me during one of the interviews we were constantly being granted.

'Very well – it's more than I've ever received a week in my life.'

'Oh fancy! For most Rehabilitees it's a drop in wages. Just sign here to show you've had an interview. I've got a most fearful headache. It's not long since I had a nervous breakdown, you know.'

'Oh, you poor thing. I'd go home and have a nice long rest if I were you.'

Back at the Cuckoo Shop, I was appalled to find that my first job was to be assembling Muppet boxes. Muppets, as you may know, are ghastly google-eyed puppets with pseudo-American accents. Regularly they appeared in bright colours on the Meadowvale telly, to the delight of almost everyone except myself. I saw them as the last word in banality, and my resentment at having to provide the dratted creatures with cardboard homes may have influenced me in a mysterious fashion. For try as I might, cutting and folding the sheets of cardboard, I couldn't make a Muppet box to save my life. Everyone else felt very smug and superior about this, and Concorde patted me on the back with a few words of encouragement.

Exasperated, Mr Petherington put me on to metal mousetrap making. This seemed rather sharp on my fingers. Boldly, I confronted my supervisor.

'Sir, I can't make mousetraps, as it's against my principles to kill mice.'

Very amused by this, he set me to work pressing square blocks of dry paint into square holes in paint boxes. I found I could do this easily, and this remained my task throughout my time in the Cuckoo Shop. Once the Muppet job was done, we were all divided into mouse trappers and paint stampers. When a thousand mousetraps had been completed, they were tipped into a large wooden crate and the lid nailed down. 'For Export – East Africa' was stencilled on the crate side in the large badly-joined navy blue lettering apparently beloved by dockers and harbourmasters.

A story about the mousetraps, probably true, spread around the workshop. Before mousetraps came to Meadowvale, the convicts of Wormwood Scrubs had been entrusted with the task of making them. For a joke, the convicts who packed the traps into the crate had carefully sprung each trap, or removed its safety catch. So when the Africans at the other end prised off the lid with happy cries of 'Mousetraps! Oh goodie!' and plunged their hands inside, the scene was changed to one of horror.

'Ooyah!' they cried, like characters in the *Beano*, and danced around in pain with mousetraps hanging from their fingers. So the contract was given to Meadowvale instead.

It was true that I couldn't make mousetraps, but not for sentimental reasons. Not only have I never been able to perform mechanical tasks, but ordinary skills such as knot-tying or button-sewing-on have always eluded me. It was many years before I could dress myself, my grandparents acting as willing valets. Before coming to the Dell, I had hopes of receiving some help for these minor problems, but there appeared to be no provision made for individual matters unconnected with job-preparation. So as before, I made the best of matters, and soon became proficient at paint-pressing.

Opposite me on the same bench, hard at work without a pause, a dour, lank-haired girl, who looked like an Irish tinker, banged in block after block of paint. She had been born without a right hand, and her arm ended with a smooth natural peg shape, exactly the size of a block of paint. It was uncanny to watch her, a human machine, perfectly adapted, stamping paint cube after cube into the box, her arm swinging up and down in perfect timing. She had a fiancé in the outside world, she said, and hoped to run a café with him in Birmingham.

Meanwhile, Mr Petherington paced up and down with an eye on the production figures, growing more and more irritated. He grossly offended the fat Liverpudlian busker on one occasion.

'D'ye know what he said to me?' I was asked indignantly. 'He said I should buck up, as the Borstal boys have the same contract and each do fifty paint boxes a day! Comparing me to a Borstal Boy up for thieving, and me an invalid with a bad back! I should make a ballad of that, if I were you.'

I had become known as a writer of comic ballads on Meadowvale life, and obliged with a ditty that began:

'The Boys who come from Borstal they pack fifty paints a day,

The Boys who come from Meadowvale, they just get in the way . . .'

He read the poem over when I'd finished, and tried to hum it. In it I exhorted the Cuckoo Shop to follow the good example of the Borstal Boys, instead of selfishly insisting on going without sundry arms and legs.

'Not as good as "The Geranium Potter's Lament", but not bad,' he commented.

Suddenly a great row broke out, as a tall gangling farm boy from Wiltshire called Tom Pringle began roaring at Concorde, who looked absolutely bewildered.

'Hold me back someone, hold me back!' yelled Pringle, threshing his arms about ferociously. Mr Petherington told him to calm down, but he darkly threatened to have poor Concorde expelled as a 'bum bandit'.

Completely innocent of homo- or any other sort of sexuality, Concorde had long been in the habit of running behind people and tickling them under their arms. A worldly man, who went to Smokey Joe's, Tom Pringle had misinterpreted this and gone berserk. Poor Concorde was most distressed, and said he'd tell the vicar. He had become a member of the market town church near the Dell, and attended every Sunday.

The Yorkshireman had made friends with a very jovial, kindly old Hampshire farm worker who had been injured after falling into a bailing machine. These two now took Concorde under their collective wing and protected him from Pringle. Both the older men were very impressed by Concorde's churchgoing, and said 'Good for him!' when I told them about it. As a matter of fact, the Hampshire man said 'Good for 'ee!' but you get the idea.

At times Meadowvale resembled Babel, with its variety of accent. Geordie often joined us during tea breaks, and his tones clashed oddly with the hearty roars from Hampshire and the quiet humorous wisdom of Yorkshire.

'Ah'm sick!' he told me once.

'D'you mean you aren't well?'

'No, that's got nowt to *do* wi' it. Sick means "fed up" where Ah come from. It's reaight deid here, since my mate Chips started going out wi' Mandy. If only Ah had mah beaike [bike] Ah'd go streaight home.'

He cheered up later at the art class when an older man decorated his record box with an oil painting of a snarling red devil with pointed teeth. This box was to be fixed on the back of Geordie's motor bike, high in the moors of the Pennines where he came from, and he hoped it would make him the terror of the roads.

One Monday morning Mr Petherington seemed rather excited, as if he had something on his mind. Finally, he unburdened himself, and everyone listened with great interest.

'Yesterday I took my wife and little girl to the Safari Park for a treat, and all the way along, we kept getting overtaken by darkies! When we got there, we found all these darkies ahead of us in better cars than I've got myself!'

'That's it! That's it!' shouted the Liverpudlian, now quite in sympathy with the supervisor. An unholy glow seemed to illumine both their features.

A burly curly-haired Rehabilitee called Rod seemed very interested, and later he came over to talk to me. He was slightly lame and had a cast in one eye, after the now familiar accident. A boastful man, whose knobbly features and way of speaking reminded me of a young Arthur Scargill, he claimed to have been completely paralysed once.

'Will power, that's how I cured myself!' he would always say, 'I've an iron will, and it's all down to mind over matter.'

'All that talk about darkies, that's racism, that is,' he now informed me. 'You can't blame these darkies wanting revenge and bigger cars after we've raped their way of life. *Raped* it, you know, *raped* it! I believe in complete equality. We're equal with *them*, and *they're* equal with us. *They* should be *there* and we should be here! It's as simple as that – send them all back to where they come from.'

I continued pressing paints as impassively as the stump-handed girl. The only coloured person in Meadowvale Dell was a very glum Indian who described himself as 'a Hindu Christian'. Rod came from Hull, where he lived on a council estate with a young wife and children, his parents and grandparents living not far away. Another of his boasts was that 'oop north' in Hull, everyone believed in family life, 'real united families' and a precious load of rascals too, if you ask me.

Our Cuckoo Shop and the larger machine shop had been built rather insensitively over the terrace that once faced the ballroom windows of the manor house. The ballroom itself had long been divided into smaller rooms for psychologists and social workers, nervous beings who feared for their jobs. As bells rang, we hurried and jostled our way along narrow passages between the outbuildings. Bits of white porch and a corner of the conservatory survived among the workshops, and I was very intrigued by a strawberry tree that grew over our daily pathway, dangling berries over our heads from twisty ilex-like branches. Although these fruit looked exactly like strawberries, I don't remember seeing anybody taste them.

From clues like these it was possible to try and imagine what the Dell must have been like in its days as a private home. In my spare time, before the evenings grew too dark, I would wander around the grounds imagining chandeliers ablaze in the mansion, sending long paths of light across the lawns. At seven in the morning, I would stop, though late for breakfast, and imagine dainty footprints in the dewy grass as the maids flitted about their duties.

One day, when in pensive mood, I roamed through the rose garden, among the yew hedges, and suddenly came upon Diana the wheelchair girl sitting in her chair looking up into the face of the unspeakable Rod. He sat on a bench beside her and held her hands. As she looked up at him, her brown eyes blazed with such intense love that it almost frightened me. Starting back, I disappeared into the greenery. A great sadness stole over me, perhaps because I knew that nobody would ever look at *me* like that, and I wiped a tear from my eye. Could this be the tender pash? No, I was far too old.

Next day, Rod and Diana's engagement was the talk of the Dell, along with all the other engagements. Chips, who was about to break off his engagement with Mandy and get engaged to a girl called Vanda, was particularly shaken.

'I don't s'pose she *knows* 'e's mar-rud,' he said in broader Norfolk than usual. 'Better not tell 'er, I suppo-ose.'

I agreed, as the expression on Diana's face suggested that neither Heaven nor Hell nor all the powers therein could make her change her mind.

Soon I was concentrating hard on pressing dry paint tablets into boxes. The bell went, but I went on to finish my box.

'You on overtime or something?' an unpleasant voice enquired. It was a tall youth I disliked, who sometimes snapped at me with the metal crab-pincers that had replaced his hands.

'If you work hard, they'll expect more from all of us,' he went on to say, showing his trade union mentality. I finished my box and left, pausing as I did so to eavesdrop on Rod and Mr Petherington, who now seemed to be the best of friends.

'You've certainly landed on your feet you lucky sod!' Mr P was saying. '*She* must be worth a tidy few bob.'

'Yeah, they say 'er old man's loaded. 'E's bound to give me a cushy job when I leave.'

Disgusted, I hurried to the canteen, turning over in my mind a plan for abolishing trade unions and replacing them by a better means of ensuring that workers were fairly treated. Unions run by workers were like alcoholic homes run by alcoholics, a sure recipe for tyranny. With no unions, all strikes would be 'wildcat', the only legitimate strikes there are, as they show the men's real feelings. My long-term plan depended, as almost every scheme for the betterment of Britain must, on a restored landed class of great confidence. At regular hearings, both management and workers would seem on an equal footing to the grand dowager who surveyed them through her lorgnette. This lady and her colleagues would see themselves as a kind of RSPCA for factory workers, always there to ensure that there was no cruelty involved. 'And now my good man, is Mr Bounderby treating you *fairly*?'

My daydreams were broken when Mandy ran across the hall and gave me a friendly hug.

'I want to talk to you! About Chips!' she burst out tearfully, 'He doesn't loov me any more! He's got engaged to Vanda!'

'Oh dear, dear! How did that happen?'

'I don't know, I wish I did! Do you know what I think?'

'What's that?'

'I don't think it *is* loov he feels for her! I think it's infatuation! Do *you* think it's infatuation?'

It seemed more like battiness to me, as Vanda was a shrewish-looking girl with a vile temper, but I murmured something appropriate. Just then, Stan, the boy who liked 'electric mild', hurried by.

'You all right?' he called, the standard greeting, which seemed a little out of place here.

'I'm surviving,' she replied.

'Surviving what?' he asked in surprise, as this was the wrong answer.

'Loovsick pangs!' she shouted, with such vehemence that he jumped in mock-alarm.

Lovers of scandal could have had a field day at Meadowvale Dell, as everybody was in love with somebody. Only the old lags were exempt, and nobody I knew went near *them*. However, the fascination for drink, striptease, gambling and so on, that seemed pure and idealistic in young men of sixteen to eighteen years of age, could lead them on to becoming coarse old lags themselves in the future. As youngsters they invested so much faith and fervour in their materialism as to lift it to a loftier plane, along with their romantic notions of perpetual 'engagements'.

Earlier that very day, Nicky, who had recovered from his passion for Janice, told me very solemnly that he was engaged to Vanda.

'I knew I was engaged, as she kissed me,' he said. 'I don't think we'll have any children unless *she* wants them.'

A few hours later he was chucked, and here she was, engaged to Chips! It was very confusing.

Before chancing his luck with Diana, the unspeakable Rod, the horror of Hull, had tried to seduce Lula the Greek girl. She had turned him down, and he blamed her religion.

'See, she's got this religious "hang-up",' he explained. 'In the end she'll turn into a Lesbian or a frustrated spinster.'

Lula herself was in love with a tall handsome young man who had once been a 'roadie' for a famous pop group. 'Roadie', short for 'road manager' appears to be the title given to a pop singer's labourer, the man who carries the heavy electric equipment about and sets it up on stage. A new Mayhew is needed to describe this strange sub-world of pop employment. Anyway, Dave the Roadie had been damaged in a crash and now shook and stammered most pitifully. One day when he was feeling better, he had called me aside and asked me if I would persuade Lula to forget her religious principles.

'I can't do that! Why don't *you* remember *yours*, and ask her to marry you?'

'What, g-get married! This is real life, not a fairy tale!'

Once again, I felt glad I had never entered the nightmare world of pop music, where harshness and cynicism were the rule.

Dave the Roadie was part of an 'intellectual set' that included a long-haired Irish youth called Columb, who had haemophilia, and a mysterious and arty girl called Marion, who dabbled in Eastern Mysticism. She spoke in a soft whispery voice like cream dropping from a jug. Columb belonged to a cult who worshipped a boy guru. Dave's pop group, too, had been 'intellectual', a bunch of former schoolteachers who tried to sing blues like American Negroes. This set was pleasant enough in its slightly superior way, but I felt I had more in common with the younger Rehabilitees, Chips, Mandy and company.

One romance that seemed to end successfully was between Mick, a former motorbike boy, and Annie, a Lowland Scots girl with an enchanting accent. Mick suffered from partial loss of memory, and would sit alone at mealtimes, looking crestfallen and sad. A very innocent country girl, Annie began to keep him company, and soon Mick was smiling from ear to ear, hardly able to believe his luck. I think they really *did* get married, so fairy tales can come true.

Curiously enough, fairies, their existence or otherwise, were quite a talking point with many Meadowvale youngsters. They referred to them as the 'little people', and while some poured scorn on the idea, others swore that they had met Irishmen who'd seen them. I once met an old countrywoman from the Malvern hills who said that years before she had persuaded her little daughter that fairies were dancing along the moonbeams.

'I never undeceived her, hadn't the heart. She looked hard and told me she could see them too.'

Later I had met the daughter, now a jolly council estate housewife, wheeling a pushchair, and she brought up the subject of fairies at once.

'I saw one quite clearly when I was a girl – a dear little thing, dancing in the moonlight in a frilly dress,' she said. So it seems that fairies, like their tales, can never die.

A few nights after the excitement of the various 'engagements' had died down, I was curled up snugly in bed when I heard a tap on the window. Looking out, I saw a dishevelled young woman in glasses, and asked her what she wanted.

'Don't mind me, I'm the cook, so I am,' she replied in an Irish accent. 'I'm just nosing round. Will you let me in? It's raining out here.'

Wondering whatever a cook could want at that time of night, I hurried down to the end of the barracks, where the door could be opened from the inside. The penalty for entertaining a girl overnight was expulsion, so I felt apprehensive. To my alarm, the cook followed me back to my room, and sat on a chair, staring at me. Too late, I realised she was a mentally disturbed Rehabilitee.

'There's no love in England,' she remarked suddenly.

'No more there is,' I agreed firmly. 'Let's go for a walk.'

Meekly she followed me along the corridor and allowed herself to be shown outdoors. It wasn't very chivalrous of me, but next day I heard that the girl had been returned to a mental home, after banging at various windows, so I suppose she had been put to bed in the end.

My own wanderings at night, which so enraged the old lags, mostly consisted of visits to the toilet and back. One night I emerged and found five upturned drawing pins outside my door, but I carefully walked round them.

A fussy, officious Welsh supervisor would upset the lags terribly, by ordering them to 'Turn off that radio!' I slept in the same row as the rough-looking ex-prisoners, as I was about the same age as them. We were worlds apart, but in the end I pleased them with a 'Ballad of the Welsh Pig', as they called the supervisor. It was a fact that this strutting supervisor, who saw that we were all in bed at night, ate several dinners one after the other in the canteen. He would gobble his food quickly, and then run back to the queue again. To me he wasn't too bad a fellow, but then I accepted petty authority with amusement, unlike the easily-outraged lags. After the Ballad was composed, they treated me with great civility, and I later saw my work pinned to the canteen wall.

Someone who amused the lags was Concorde, who wandered down our corridor one day, proudly holding a pocket calculator that his parents had given him. When we worked together in the garden, he had used it to count beans and geraniums. Now he was adding up the numbers on all our doors, going up and down the rows.

'The total number is one thousand nine hundred and eighteen!' he announced in triumph. When I praised him, he frisked like a puppy. A most welcome visitor.

My next job was in the office. The object of all the chopping and changing was to see which job suited us the best. Unlike school career officers, who sees only three jobs in the world, factory, shop and office, the Meadowvale staff saw things differently. Here it was gardening, factory and office. I now had to endure office work for the first time in my life. This was the work my grammar school teachers had recommended for me.

'Kerridge might settle down as an accounts clerk in some out of the way branch of the Electricity Board,' my family had been told.

Seeking a second opinion, my grandfather had taken me to a school leavers' career office. There they had suggested shops. I explained that I was unable to do anything with numbers, and insisted on working in a factory. This had enraged the man. He had worn a brown suit, I remember, and now his face turned purple.

'You can't work in a factory if you've been to grammar school!' he roared.

Nevertheless, I stuck to my guns, and in a spirit of revenge, he found me a job in a backstreet wire weaving firm, where I was placed among boys of fifteen fresh from secondary modern schools, earning two pounds and a penny a week. That was at the close of the class-obsessed nineteen fifties. My sole reason for wanting to work in a factory was so that I could write a novel about it. Influenced and inflamed by the Joan Littlewood stable of writers who were then my heroes, I imagined that every novel had to be a 'working-class novel'. Therefore before you could write a novel, you had to make yourself working-class. After a week of trying unsuccessfully to weave wire, I decided I was working-class enough, the seal on my proletarianism having been set by

Kingsley Martin, editor of the *New Statesman*, who had accepted the first of my essays. This desire of pupils to become 'working-class' helped to undo the poor old grammar schools, as it pulled their foundation from under them. It resulted first of all in a 'new class' of grammar school boys doing workmen's jobs which didn't suit them, and which caused them to curse at 'capitalism'. Then it led to Comprehensive Schools and the modern generation of sub-working-class young people who want to be genteel and go in for wine and foreign restaurants. I am firmly of the egg-and-chips-and-a-cuppa grammar school breed, and cannot understand the modern ways at all.

So here I was in an office! Dennis, the whispering boy, really *was* cut out to be a clerk, and was already doing wonders in a streamlined Portakabin office where everyone rattled and donged at typewriters. Perhaps because of the results of my IQ test, I was put in a sleepier 'firm' in a yellow painted room full of hotwater pipes in the basement of the mansion. Diana of the wheelchair was there, but I felt rather shy of her since seeing her with Rod. She had grown very friendly with a kind, gentle old fellow with a bald head, whom she called 'Primrose'. I don't know why he was there. Every time she called him by his nickname, he blushed most becomingly.

Our work consisted of checking everybody's number and making sure that leavers' names were crossed off various charts, and newcomers' names and numbers filled in. A great deal of playing with numbers went on at the Dell, and every now and then a Rehabilitee would be summoned to some office by a loudspeaker proclaiming, 'May I have your attention please!'

This was more of a command than a question, and it would end in someone being asked if their number had been quoted correctly somewhere.

By concentrating hard, I could do the work, but I was glad I hadn't taken my teacher's advice, all those years before. When I was given more difficult tasks, I grew so dismayed that they were taken away again, which was certainly an improvement on school. Whenever he could, Rod would pop in to see Diana, and during tea breaks he would give her walking lessons. It seemed clear to me that she would never walk again and that to make her try was a form of torture. But it was no use telling that to Rod.

'All it needs is will power!' he would shout, as she fell yet again, to be caught in his brawny arms. 'I done it and so can you! I was worse that you – it was my faith in myself that made me walk. Be strong! Be strong! It's an inflexible will you need, strength of will, mind over matter! Be strong!'

'I – I can't, Rod! I can't walk!'

'There, you silly cow, you nearly fell over again! That's because you said "I can't"! There's no such word as bloody "can't"! You *can*! You should say to yourself "I *can*."'

All this was very distressing for the lookers-on, who didn't know what to think. A strong will can be useful, but so can acceptance of one's limitations. I was always a sucker for the latter approach. Sometimes when I was a boy, grown-ups would say, 'You only *think* you can't do this because you lack confidence. Of course you can really do it! Just say to yourself, "I can do it!"'

Amazed, I would think 'Perhaps I really *can* do it! They're grown up and might know better than me. They say I can do it, and so I'll try.'

A terrible catastrophe would then ensue, as whatever it was, I couldn't do it at all. So ever since I've been a grown-up myself, I've been a firm believer in 'can't'.

Not surprisingly, Diana grew unhappy, and made arrangements to leave the Dell.

'What's the use of it here?' she asked me. 'They don't teach you anything sensible. Why did they bother to admit half the people here, when it's clear they can never work again? Even when one leaves they can only recommend one for a certain type of job. They can't *provide* a job at all.'

'Well, I look on it as a social club where you can meet nice people,' I said. 'What sort of work do you want to do?'

'Write poetry, actually.'

'There you are, it's excellent training! You can write tragic poetry if you like.'

'Um,' she said dubiously, but reached for her notebook.

'For Rod – Why I love you,' I read over her shoulder.

One Rehabilitee whose career was being helped was a sly-looking man from Northern Ireland, who once confided in me that he was really a professor of Sociology, out to write a series of articles exposing the Dell.

'Don't give away my secret!' he chuckled. 'Last night I volunteered for the mathematics class. It was incredible! They treated grown men as five year olds, and began with "two and two is four." '

'I prefer to look on all this as Fiction,' I replied austerely.

Fortunately, I was soon taken out of the office, and my last ten days at Meadowvale Dell were spent doing a job I really enjoyed, Running Messages. For this I had my own office, as it were, a lone desk and chair in the middle of the mansion's Gothic hall. No armour stood against the walls now, but a huge fireplace remained with twisting leaves in the stonework around it. A fine oak staircase curved its way to lofty regions where supervisors may have lived in splendour, for some of the staff lived on the premises. Behind me, in a huge office, the nervous, silly but good-natured social worker held sway among the files. A great wooden siege-proof door in front of me sheltered the staff psychologist. A confident man, of the 'good, fine, great, great!' variety, he enjoyed long lunches and went out a great deal. My job was to run from workshop to workshop and fetch people for interviews with these two.

Swelling with importance, the job going to my head, I would interrupt a class, deferred to by all, call out a name and lead the interviewee back to headquarters. Newcomers to the Dell seemed to take me for a headmaster, and trotted behind me fearfully and respectfully.

'Don't worry, they won't eat you,' I would assure the victims loftily and unconvincingly.

By now I had already written a part of this book, 'The Summer of 'Seventy-Seven'. I gave it to the psychologist to read.

'It's good for you to write down your feelings and let off steam,' he said benignly, and put the manuscript into his briefcase.

Every few days I would ask him what he thought of it, and each time he'd say that he hadn't actually begun it. Soon I began to ask him for it back, but he could never lay his hands on it. One happy day, when I was about to leave the Dell, I saw my manuscript on his desk, while he was at lunch in the nearby town. I swiped it back and he never mentioned it to me again.

An odd Rehabilitee I had to deal with at this time was a new boy who had recently been released from an asylum. He resembled a giant spider monkey, with long arms and legs and a bullet head with dark eyes and eyebrows. His limbs were completely double jointed, and would swing rapidly inwards and outwards as if he were a string puppet out of control. His moods would suddenly vary from exhilaration to savage anger and back again, and if he were crossed, by being given an order, he would chatter his teeth in rage. I was afraid he would injure someone, not least myself, and advised every supervisor I saw to send him away again.

Listening at the psychologist's door, I was flattered to hear my name mentioned as someone who thought the monkey-man couldn't be Rehabilitated here. Next moment I had the unnerving task of fetching the man himself for an examination. He followed me affably enough, and sat on a bench near the psychologist's door waiting to be called. Then he lit a cigarette, and the social worker calmly told him to put it out again, before vanishing behind her door.

At once he began to swear, jump and gibber.

'Be quiet!' I ordered him, and to my surprise he obeyed and merely muttered. After his examination, he returned to his workshop, but disappeared on the following day.

All too soon my splendid position of power as Messenger was ended, and for my last two days at the Dell, I raked leaves in the garden, looking deflated. Those who had once been impressed by me laughed heartily.

*

As most Rehabilitees were lame and far from home, the nearby market town became our weekend centre of activities. Some preferred pubs and others churches, but if the weather was fine I liked to walk in the woods surrounding Pompada Towers. Conifer plantations bordered by silver birches gave way to ancient oak forests that formed a mysterious background to Smokey Joe's pub. Along the red brick demesne wall that surrounded the Pompada college, chestnuts spread their foliage, bunches of leaves like spokes in endless cogwheels soaring up forever. Broken lodge houses and huge gate posts with iron hinges standing alone among brambles spoke of a vanished squirearchy. I loved to trespass on part of the original Dell estate that had been sold to a farmer. From the barracks, it still appeared to be one park, but a wire fence, easily climbed, separated us from an artificial lake, overgrown and full of moorhens, and from another poplar avenue leading nowhere. Two lines of poplars guarded a path that ended abruptly in a meadow where Friesians grazed. As the grounds of the Dell seemed older than the house, I liked to picture the original mansion at the head of this overgrown driveway.

Every tree and bush in the woods rustled with wildlife, and grey squirrels and jays were everywhere. The further among the trees I strayed, squishing my way among mouldy leaves, the more the squirrels seemed to resent my presence. One grew positively outraged at my intrusion and followed me swearing copiously, bounding from tree to tree. When he swore, he would hang head downwards on a tree trunk, his hind legs spreadeagled and his tail hanging down over his ears.

'Chuck chuck chuck chuck!' he raved angrily, like Donald Duck.

The jays on the other hand, were Nature's gentlemen, and received me courteously. Bouncing about among the oak roots, they competed with the squirrels for fallen acorns. I will never forget entering a glade among silver birches and seeing a jay floating down to the ground like a black, blue and white chestnut leaf.

These woods, interspersed by villas, stretched down the hill to the market town below Meadowvale. Here could be found an Anglican church, a Pentecostal fellowship, and, in a nearby hamlet, a Methodist chapel. All three ministers, to their credit, collected Rehabilitees in vans and took them to their services.

Most popular were the Pentecostalists, and Lula the Greek girl looked forward passionately to Sundays. She tried to rope in as many of us as she could, her eyes shining. When I first arrived at the Dell, she came over to talk to me at once, mistaking my Everyman George Borrow for a Bible.

Concorde came along to the 'Pentes' once, but seemed more amused than anything else by the emotional pleas for sinners to step forward. He was a staunch Anglican, helped by the fact that he remained forever on the right side of his teens. Adolescence is the best time for being 'saved', while childhood is the time to appreciate age-old rituals. One of the most pitiful sights I saw at one of Lula's meetings was when a girl called Susan, hideously mangled in a car crash, went forward and made gurgling noises to indicate her love for Jesus. She had once been a fashion model. Lacking a hall of their own, the Pentecostalists used a back room of the Town Hall. A most grandiose Palladian-looking building from the front, the Town Hall changed from white stone to brown brick as soon as you slipped round the corner, down a side alley, and through a brown door into a brown room with a stage and peeling plaster. Here the Pentecostalists met, low on appearance and intellect, but kind-hearted on the whole, and saints to some of the eager Rehabilitees.

The main speaker was normally a red-faced countryman in a check suit, a robust, roaring fellow in his thirties, with such an expression of squint-eyed villainous hypocrisy that I almost laughed aloud. It was a face I had seen drawn by Gilray, even in the artist's day suggesting a person of an earlier time, someone perhaps given to stabling horses in York Minster. Roaring coarsely on matters most holy, grinning like a Toby jug and stamping his feet, the Sturdy Rogue, helped by a wan pianist, steered the service on its way.

Dennis the clerk took these meetings most solemnly, whispering prayers for his voice to be made audible. We were encouraged to ask

God for our needs, and an equally earnest young townsman in a grey suit pleaded most piteously, with an anguished expression on his face.

'Oh Lord, please tell me what is wrong with my computer, for Lord, only You know. Please get it to work again!'

However, the last time I attended a Town Hall meeting, I was genuinely moved. Lula had rehearsed a song, 'How Great Thou Art', a very ordinary ditty in most cases. In a long white dress she walked slowly to the centre of the stage, and as her pure voice soared in song, the dingy backroom seemed to melt away. Hands clasped, she poured her heart out, and the room seemed to fill with light, the shadows vanished and we were seated in a Greek Orthodox cathedral of the utmost splendour, candles in chandeliers, statues of saints looking on and heavenly incense everywhere.

The song ended, and the Healing Service began. No Meadowvale people stood up to be cured, afraid of breaking the magical spell. With a reassuring chuckle, the Sturdy Rogue laid ham-like hands on a man with 'a bit of a stiff back' and a girl with a sore throat. Behold, they were both cured and we all went home happily.

My favourite Dell church was that of the Methodists. Kindly, gentle and middle-class, they seemed more relaxed and more genuinely Christian than many Anglicans. After the service, we would sit drinking coffee in the minister's front room, while housewives talked of sewing and bird-tables, in an atmosphere of mildness I had not known before among chapel folk. One prayer, 'Forgive us our wealth in the midst of poverty', was a little *too* Anglican for me.

Concorde and I were the only Dell visitors to the Anglican church. It was a pleasure to go there with him, as he hopped with joy, a shocked expression only coming over his face as we passed another ex-Anglican church now used as a store room for a bearded antique dealer. In these sad days for the C. of E., I attend services in the same mournful spirit as a Catholic might have done just after the Reformation. Our vicar was very fond of Youth.

In order to cater for the supposed needs of this new deity, he was tearing out the inside of the Georgian crypt to replace it by the shrine known as a Youth Club. Concorde was eagerly helping the workmen by carrying chunks of rubble about. The crypt was entered by way of a creaky door with an open rose window of twirly ironwork set in it. Inside was a maze of brick tunnels with rows of small wooden doors, like the cells of monks belonging to a subterranean Order. Each door had a name on and inside each cell or grotto, great oak coffins reposed grimly on rows of shelves. A mystic place, where I coughed reverently over the dust of ages.

'In those days the church raised money for repairs by selling vaults to families hereabouts', the callow vicar explained. 'The nuisance is that we're not allowed to tear them out until we've traced the owners' living relatives and asked for permission to remove the coffins.'

Those old dark coffins seemed to have no connection with the modern world at all. Long may their occupants remain there, forgotten by relatives, until the trumpet blast shall drown the sound of the Youth Club discotheque.

Back at the Dell, Nicky boasted of his exploits in Smokey Joe's, and derided us for going to church.

'I used to believe in God, right? But then look what happened! I became an epileptic.'

'You can't say, "Look God, I'll believe in you, and in return you won't give me epilepsy," ' I said. 'There's something wrong with that argument.'

A few days later, Nicky was boasting about his drinking exploits to a circle of friends. 'Well, as I was saying, I came back from Smokey Joe's after lunch paralytic, I tell you! Was I drunk! First I fell off my chair, then I began to sing!'

'Was that before or after you took all your clothes off and danced on the table?' I asked innocently.

The boy's face fell and everyone gathered around him looked delighted.

'Did I do that?' he asked.

'Yes!' everybody chorussed.

My Liverpudlian friend proved most inventive, supplying many convincing details.

'We dressed you afterwards,' Chips explained.

'But how did you get my jeans back on?'

'I held you straight, and Mandy pulled them on.'

'*Mandy*! Flipping 'eck, there was girls there! Oh, strewth! I'll never touch another drop.'

Some of us thought of letting him suffer, but after two days of leading a haunted life, Nicky looked so piteous that I confessed it had been a joke. He was more relieved than annoyed.

'I'd never of forgiven myself in front of girls!' he gasped. To cheer himself up, he stayed out late at Smokey Joe's to see the strip-tease, giving a secret signal on his return for Chips to sneak him in.

Diana, the wheelchair girl, left a week before the rest of us.

'Daddy's still in Suffolk shooting, but he's sending his chauffeur to fetch me,' she said. Mandy too left early, after a tearful row with Vanda, a tough, dark-haired girl from Workington, who had a crooked arm.

'What have you done to my Chips?' she had demanded. 'You've stolen his affections!'

Vanda swung her arm and hit Mandy on the jaw. Screaming, Mandy ran to a supervisor, who sheltered her. Meanwhile, Vanda stomped around the canteen and gym looking for Mandy, growling with rage and asking for her everywhere. Chips hid, in company with a new girl who swiftly became engaged to him.

Instead of curbing Vanda, the authorities decided to send Mandy home.

'Goodbye, I hope you never find what loov is like,' she gasped, and then ran frantically for the station mini bus. 'Wait for me!'

'If anyone lays a ha-and on moy new girl friend, man or woman, I'll *flatten* 'em!' Chips declared.

However, his new love, a beefy girl, was well able to take care of herself. She felled Vanda with a blow and ended up by knocking down Chips himself.

The quiet day-girl who had been going out with the 'electric mild' man suffered a severe breakdown when she found he had been unfaithful to her. She was sent to a nearby mental hospital, and as soon as I could I went to see her.

This hospital, now under threat of closure, had been built by the Aqua Pompada man, a hundred years ago. It towered above the road, a vast Gothic edifice, resembling the Arthurian castle in the Doré woodcut. Set in stately grounds, the hospital had been intended for the distracted nobility. Inside, my footsteps echoed in the oversized halls, where large individual rooms took the place of wards. Connected in pairs, the rooms had been meant both for a patient and for his valet. Meeting the girl, Stephanie, in the cafeteria, I remarked on these wonders. The café itself resembled the oldest parts of the Kremlin, with ornately carved wooden pillars painted in patterns of flowers and hunting scenes.

'That's nothing, let me show you the ballroom,' said Stephanie, who seemed much better.

I followed her up an enormous staircase, stepping over an old man who lay prostate on a landing, crying his eyes out.

'Take no notice, he always does that,' my guide informed me. 'Now this is the ballroom. We still sometimes have dances here.'

Huge dark crimson velvet curtains hung across the windows. In the dim light I walked along the polished floor gazing at gigantic oil paintings of English monarchs. The work of a noble inmate in Victorian times, the paintings, in gilt frames, seemed eerie and Elizabethan. Queen Elizabeth the First herself wore a long crinkly yellow gown covered in human eyes. Staring blue eyes, with lashes complete, peered back at me from the folds of her garments. I didn't care for this, and made my goodbyes and left. Stephanie, I heard, soon recovered, despite the eyes.

One by one the 'intake' I had arrived with at Meadowvale Dell departed for their various homes. Lula left, and so did Concorde, both giving me their addresses and urging me to visit them. It was now

November, Christmas was approaching, and spurred on by a friendly supervisor, some of the Rehabilitees were rehearsing for an end-of-term show.

Roaming in the garden one evening, I was surprised to hear a haunting fiddle tune swirling from one of the tiny barracks windows. Peeping through, I saw, to my surprise, the tall bespectacled farm boy, Tom Pringle from Wiltshire. With a violin tucked under his chin, he was squinting slightly in concentration, as he played a sprightly dance tune.

'I'm going to play the "Londonderry Air" for the concert,' he later told me.

'Are you a musician, then?' I asked in surprise, remembering his unkind treatment of Concorde.

'No, it's only a hobby. My real ambition is to be a pig man. At this farm I was on, before I was ill, they let me use the electric cattle prods to get the pigs up the ramp into the market van. Coo, they did squeal! I like pigs – they've got character.'

The day of the Show soon arrived and Tom Pringle played his piece to an audience of old lags and supervisors, who clapped politely. Most of the younger crowd had left, but Nicky, Chips, and Geordie sat together in the audience. 'Electric Mild' got up and sang a pop song unaccompanied, which was well received.

But to my surprise, an old lag I had never noticed before, an East Ender called Ernie, was the star of the Show. He came on dressed as a vicar, to howls of laughter from the audience. The Liverpudlian busker and the supervisor, Mr Petherington, acted as straight men, and attempted to interview him. After reciting the Trade Unionist's prayer, 'Each day thou shalt do no labour and on the seventh thou shalt claim for overtime,' the 'vicar' pulled out a bottle of beer, swigged from it deeply and said 'F— me, that was good!'

A latent anti-clericalism rose from the audience, who laughed so much they nearly burst. Chips and Nicky went bright red choking with laughter, stamping and slapping their thighs. Geordie smiled in a restrained way and Dennis the whispering boy looked pained. I put on a long-suffering but indulgent expression. The show ended with hardened old housebreakers in hysterics, as the 'vicar' pulled a pair of knickers out of his pocket, said 'f—' several times and referred to 'mothers' meetings', 'Dearly beloved brethren' and 'going out and getting pissed after Evensong'.

No act could follow this, and the show came to a tumultuous end, the 'vicar' being cheered and slapped on the back wherever he went, always referred to as 'the Rev'. Trying, in the medieval manner, to see an allegory in all that occurred, I decided that the Show represented the Ideal of the Church of England, Getting the Common Touch. Like the Midas touch, it might do more harm than good, if achieved.

Partings, partings! Bags were now being packed, and the plastic paper-knives went on sale to their makers. Chips had given his knife a horse-head handle, and Geordie's handle was shaped like a bird. My knife had a handle on both ends.

'Ah feel reaight huffed that mah mum's collecting me as if Ah were a wain,' Geordie announced, to our initial bafflement.

Chips fussed around a new girl friend, carrying her bags as well as his own. Every now and then his illness caused him to double up in agony, but he always straightened himself and smiled anew, roaring out a joke or a boast. Dennis the whisperer went to have a last look at the path. Our mini bus arrived and we were off. Had our stay at Meadowvale Dell been a waste of time? Opinions varied. Those who had expected to be trained for a specific job and to have a job interview granted on leaving, were disappointed and bitter. Others had been dole drawers, who turned jobs down, and had been sent to the Dell as a last chance by the DHSS. Now their dole would be secure for a long time, and they were glad. Most of us, particularly the younger ones, just looked on it as an adventure in itself, and now looked forward to the next treat life had to offer. Often the most hideously mutilated were the most optimistic, a lesson for us all.

Laughing, the victims of motorbike accidents fenced noisily with their crutches or snapped at one another with their artificial hands. If Meadowvale had taught me one thing it was that all the motorbikes in the world should be heaped up and made into a bonfire. However, God looked down from His window in the sky and saw what was going on. Somehow or another, the British and the Americans lost the ability to make motorbikes. Perhaps the much maligned trade unions were the cause of this. If so, they have their uses. As I write, the only motorbikes on sale at first hand are light Japanese models, similar to the once-derided motor scooters. Hard core motorbike boys spend their time buying up old bikes and re-vamping them, becoming mechanics rather than suicides in the process. So passed that enemy of mankind, the motorbike.

Before I left, I was called in to meet the social worker. With some ceremony, she handed me a type of diploma to take to the Jobcentre.

'We try and find what each Rehabilitee is best suited for,' she told me. 'Often Rehabilitees don't know what they're best at themselves until the psychologists and supervisors find out for them. We have recommended you here as a lavatory attendant or a messenger.'

So my days spent as the Meadowvale messenger had not been unappreciated.

In the years that followed I made every effort to find out what my fellow Rehabilitees were doing, and to keep in touch. Chips joined the Army and became a Gunner for a time, before his slight disability was discovered. Then he was given a safer job, and like most soldiers, he lost no time in getting married. He and Mrs Chips now live in the married quarters at Catterick.

Diana the wheelchair girl moved into a flat in her sister's house in Kensington, and Rod from Hull moved in with her. The flat had been specially adapted for her wheelchair, and she was skilled at keeping house while Rod worked as a dustman. She soon grew to hate him, and told me in bitter tones that 'Class is the most important thing in the world.'

Most 'living togethers' last for three years, and at the end of that time, much swollen with meat and drink, Rod returned to Hull.

Mandy, much to Lula's delight when I told her, became a 'born again Christian'. She is not working, but the social life of 'Youth Christianity' keeps her in a whirl of activity, and she is currently engaged to a 'born again' ex – Hell's Angel called Wilfred. He works as a vacuum cleaner salesman in Carlisle.

Concorde, cared for by his devoted parents, found a job working in a convent garden. When I go and see him, I find him standing at the top of his road staring at everyone who passes until he recognises me with a wild shout.

Dennis the whispering boy, became a clerk in earnest, in a factory office, and works hard and diligently. He too had been 'born again', but despite his prayers his voice is still not very loud.

Geordie helps in his father's garage at a tiny lost village in the mountains. It is not a fulltime job, but it keeps him happy. Although he has not grown, his appearance is manly and he drives around in a car, drinking lager out of tins and listening to a horrendous type of pop music called 'Heavy Metal'. Fans seem required to wear black T-shirts with brightly coloured pictures on them, obscene, violent or grotesque, and covered in glittering spangles. Thus attired, Geordie looks a bit odd in his parents' immaculate stone cottage, but he seems more cheerful and boisterous than in his Meadowvale days. His friendship with Chips, whom he still sees, must have done him good.

Lula is still pining for Dave the Roadie, and works as a dentist's receptionist. I bullied Dave into writing to her. He promised he'd call on her, but didn't. However, she is still a Pentecostalist, and invited me to an enormous week-long Pente-rally at Butlin's Holiday Camp, Minehead. There, among the playful, flirtatious crowds of young people, she seemed to be in her element.

Nicky, bright-looking in his peak-faced way at seventeen, has grown up big and oafish. When I last saw him, he steered me into a pub.

'This is a dangerous place, but watch me and do everything I do, and you'll be all right,' he warned me as we entered.

Inside, it seemed to be a perfectly ordinary pub, with a friendly middle aged landlady. Nicky walked around the bar asking elderly customers to lend him money. They seemed indulgent towards him, but I didn't like to copy him in case I received rougher treatment.

No mention was made of scaffolding, and Nicky's mother told me that he was obviously unfit to work.

I never saw the honest Yorkshireman again; and that's all I can tell you of my friends at the Dell.

Last year, with tender memories of the friendships I had made at the Dell, of the ridiculous but well-meaning staff there and of the haunting, half ruined Victorian garden, I revisited the place. Taking my seat at the usual desk in the newspaper room, I noticed only unshaven old lag types around me. There were no bright young motorbike casualties or romantically minded girls at all. It was evening, and most of the staff had gone home. Everything in the grounds seemed the same, from the strawberry tree to the white statue in its little bower. I looked down at the red roofs of the kitchen garden towards Smokey Joe's and the forest beyond. Halfway down the hill, near the compost heap, lay the stone path that whispering Dennis and I had made. It was as good as new.

[PART FOUR]
Our Man in St Mungo's

One day I was reading the newspapers when an item seemed to spring from the page towards me, the newsprint flashing in neon colours while sirens went off and pound note signs lit up in my eyes.

'Georgette Heyer Memorial Prize,' I read. 'To commemorate the late Georgette Heyer, a prize of £500 is being offered for the best historical novel. The winning novel will be published. Send off for details to . . .'

'Quick, get me pencil and paper!' I shouted to my mother, whose hospitality I was enjoying. Ideas for the novel poured into my mind. Recently there had been a series of programmes on BBC Television about a reconstructed Iron Age village, where hapless students attempted to survive using Celtic farm implements. Soay sheep, an old Celtic breed, had been placed at their mercy. In some quarters, this misguided endeavour had been taken very seriously as a clue to what prehistoric village life may have been like. As the volunteers were somewhat hippie-like, the scheme may have owed its inspiration to a vague idea that rebels and nonconformists are Children of Nature, able to lead us back to the Dawn of the Gods. The bemused young people had been told to perform pagan fire rituals whose meaning they could not understand.

To my way of thinking, the television people had put the cart before the horse, or the chariot before the Icelandic pony. Divine inspiration comes first in any people's history, and without the gods of the Celts, the huts, ploughs and spinning wheels of the time would be as empty of meaning as the BBC's religious ceremony. So my novel, which I decided to call *Druid Madonna*, would put first things first, and deal with Iron Age life from a religious point of view. No one knew very much about the religious practices of the pre-Roman Celts, so I could make up anything I liked. Georgette Heyer would have been proud of me, I felt, as I wrote page after page, my right hand alive with the tingly feeling of Fiction. As far as I know, Miss Heyer, whose works I have not yet read, has never tackled the prehistoric period. My private reading, in which I had tried to trace the King Arthur stories back to their earliest source, had led me into some strange and haunted byways. Every half-remembered ballad or legend was grist to my mill, and as my preparatory notes took shape, they took the form of an oak tree, with roots, trunk and spreading branches. This was accidental, unless it was a sign from the Druids, and I took it as a good omen.

Soon my story was finished, complete with a Christian message, and I was faced with another problem. How to get it typed out? A secretarial agency, where my handwriting was understood, offered to do the job for twenty pounds. This seemed an impossibly large sum for me to obtain at that time. My grandparents had once sent me to typing lessons. There the same thing had occurred as at my riding lessons of earlier years. I started off fairly well, and then just when my teacher was beginning to be pleased with me, I forget everything I had ever learned. To attempt anything practical, I now knew from past experience, was futile. Pondering, I took the bus back to the scenes of my lavatory triumphs, a painted stone in my pocket.

For some time I had been painting goggle-eyed animals on pebbles from Pupworth beach, and hawking them around the souvenir shops. A black shiny piece of knapped flint proved an ideal background for a vivid poster colour picture, which then looked like a 'cel' for a Disney cartoon. Disney artists used to paint their characters on celluloid. The shiny mottled surface of a Sussex flint may have resembled this material, and it was certainly a delight to work on. When completed, the painting could be varnished and it would seem a part of the stone. Some shopkeepers paid me up to a pound for each picture.

My search for new, untried souvenir shops led me down to the river, where houseboats were moored in the mud, some slowly sinking to oblivion along with the retired seafarers, young part-time fishermen, tramps and burnt-out hippies who lived in them. A cocky young gipsyish lad, a lurcher by his side, sat on the edge of a boat and chatted to a lank-haired woman with a child.

'Yeah, I got to go for an identification parade. Three blokes mugged someone on the train last night. Put it like this, I get a pound for going. Watch out, young lady – my dog'll have your hand off! I get five pounds a day working three hours mending boats, get dole on top and sleep on the boat for nothing, so I'm well away; can't complain.'

Hearing of these riches emboldened me, so while the woman's little girl stroked the dog, which licked her tenderly, I offered its master a flint portrait of a pink donkey with a fish's tail.

'What do I want with that?' he enquired, not unnaturally. 'I know who'd buy it. Go in that shop with the stripes on, The Gift Box. It's just the sort of thing they like.'

I took his advice, and entered the shop with the stripy awning. A tall well-built young man with a cheerfully innocent expression approached me, and I showed him the stone. To my surprise, he gave a shout of joy and called his wife over to see it.

'Can you do more of those?' he asked, after paying me thirty pence in cash.

'Certainly. How many do you want?'

'If you can do a hundred, I'll pay you twenty pounds.'

'How much?'

'Twenty pounds.'

'Done!'

This was the finest business deal I had ever made. I had to work hard, as the time limit for the competition was running out. By concentrating to the utmost, I could do six stones in a day. Locked in my room and working furiously, I reached my target and took a heavy, clinking bagfull to The Gift Box, whose owner proved as good as his word. So the typing lady was paid, *Druid Madonna* was typed, and (metaphorically speaking) the pig went over the stile and the old woman got home that night. I had done it! My first historical novel was now on its way to the Georgette Heyer people, leaving me proud but exhausted.

Was Rod at Meadowvale Dell right after all? Could a strong will conquer all? No, because if it could, I would have been able to type, and the twenty pounds would not have been needed. As regards *Druid Madonna* and the painted stones, I preferred to recall the words of George Borrow in *Lavengro*, which oft have given me hope, courage and the strength to go on. In adverse circumstances, Borrow had written an historical novel, *The Life of Joseph Sell*, and found a publisher for it. No copy now exists, but I see no reason to doubt him: 'Before I departed I received the twenty pounds, and departed with a light heart to my lodgings. Reader, amidst the difficulties and dangers of this life, should you ever be tempted to despair, call to mind these latter chapters of the life of Lavengro. There are few positions, however difficult, from which dogged resolution and perseverance may not liberate you.'

My exhilaration was only slightly dampened by the fact that *Druid Madonna* failed ignominiously to win the Georgette Heyer Memorial Prize, and was promptly sent back to me again. Luckily, I had enclosed a stamped addressed envelope. However, I felt very pleased with my story, as I thought that my knowledge of West Africans had helped me to understand the Celtic mind. My faith was justified four years later, when 'Druid Madonna' was published by the Brynmill Press of Retford.

From time to time, I felt a twinge of sadness at the death of my tramp friend Jim, together with indignation at the authorities for 'returning him to the Community'. Eventually I wrote an article about it and, on an impulse, sent it to the *Daily Telegraph*, although I had received nothing but rejection slips from that paper before. To my amazement, the article was accepted, and appeared in the celebrated 'Personal View' column! I travelled up to Fleet Street and, greatly overawed, met Morrison Halcrow, the grave Scottish features editor, and gave him a painted stone. This was my first ever piece to be printed in a daily newspaper. I received two or three sympathetic letters from readers who had worked with mental patients and knew the cruel 'returning to the Community' rule only too well. Feeling that perhaps rebelliousness, crankiness and the search for novelty were on the run at last, I decided that I should spend a week in Fleet Street and tout my articles around.

Normally, when staying in London, I lived with a West Indian family I knew. The drawback to this was that I'd sit talking with them all morning, and then spend all afternoon exploring the exciting part of London in which they dwelled. Wherever I stayed in London, I found it hard to get up in the morning and still harder, with so many alleys and by-ways to explore, to reach a specific destination. This time I would have to stay near Fleet Street itself, at the Strand, and refrain from wandering on into the East End until I had peddled my literary wares. It was the month of October, in 1979, and I felt that destiny was calling me.

The evening before my departure, I stood on the concrete bridge over the Crum, the stream which sometimes burst its artificially-straightened banks and returned Pupworth to the marshy days when Saxons had first sailed inland from the coast. Miller's Down, which dominated the horizon, would not have been crowned with beech trees then, but with a Roman Villa at the centre of a rebuilt Celtic fort. As I gazed, jolly ladies in Wellington boots walked by, calling their dogs. There was something cosy and Agatha Christie-ish about Pupworth, I decided. Here the nineteen thirties, that much maligned decade, had never quite ended. By now, the more cynical local children had passed on to the hell of secondary school, and a new innocent breed of mop-haired youngsters frolicked around, talking trustingly to grown-ups and playing with their dogs or fathers. Their cries grew faint as dusk drew on; a pony splashed in the shallows and an owl hooted. Horse riding was such a popular pastime that some young mothers named their children after favourite ponies. The long-suffering vicar had recently baptised a Bay Short and a Dapple Wooler. He had dissuaded Mrs Short from calling her boy 'Dun', pointing out that the name would sould like 'done short' or swindled. The riding school left the ponies out all night, chained to stakes which sometimes became uprooted and dragged around.

A last brush stroke of daylight silhouetted the mournful rows of dead elm trees against the sky. Heavy-headed horses, like strange long-legged tapirs, added a prehistoric touch to the landscape. I was only going away for a short while this time, yet I felt that events were inexorably moving me away from Pupworth. My plans were made, and these involved a saint of yesteryear.

One of my favourite saints is St Kentigern, known to his Scottish friends as Mungo the Well Beloved and to the Welsh as St Cynderin. Like St Patrick, he 'was a gentleman and came of decent people', leaving them to wander the wilds of Scotland preaching the Word. He then wandered through the Lake District and to the mountains of Wales, where he met St David. It is pleasant to think of the two saints relaxing together after a hard day's work, swapping anecdotes of the road. Crosthwaite, with its beautiful church just outside Keswick, was founded where St Kentigem planted his cross as a stand against paganism, which I imagine as a horrifying sacrifice of roaring bulls amid Beltane fires. For St Kentigern was a Celt and his mission was among Celts, Saxons being outside the Christian pale among his set in the sixth century. Avoiding Saxons may have been the saint's motive for staying in the mountains, but I like to think of him as a Christian version of the old man in *Kim*, desiring his hills. He must have had a long white beard, as he was sometimes taken for Merlin, a magician whose real life original is said to have been a Scottish bard. Under the name of Mungo, the saint is patron of the city of Glasgow. It is a little known fact, but to this very day, St Mungo gathers his children about him at the sign of the Cross. In other words, just opposite Charing Cross Station in London, facing the Strand, can be found St Mungo's hostel for men, who are mostly Scotsmen, though Saxons are not excluded. My mind aglow with the romance of St Kentigern's mission, I eagerly seized on this fact and treasured it as soon as the place was recommended to me by my tramp friend, Mr Templeton.

So I had not far to search for a Fleet Street base, nor need it concern me that Mr Halcrow's generous payment for my work had now shrunk to the fateful sum of twenty pounds. Fourteen pounds fifty pence, I found, bought me a week's accommodation, with breakfast and evening meal. For lunch, I could make use of the box of free vouchers supplied to the hostel by the Hare Krishna movement. Each ticket entitled you to a vegetarian meal at the temple near Soho Square. My creature comforts thus arranged, I felt that London was my oyster.

All the same, I felt rather daunted as I approached the hostel, which was simply the old Charing Cross Hospital put to another purpose. A noble Regency-looking building (although in fact built later) it was now grimy and down-at-heel, the paint flaking. Cross seedy-looking men dressed in black and grey lurched and skulked around the doorway. A sleepy-looking hippie and a stocky Welsh girl at the desk took my name, and to my alarm asked for my next of kin. Surely they wouldn't murder me? Looking around the bleak hall and its occupants, however, I decided that they merely feared I would die of alcoholism or T. B., as some of the others seemed to be doing. A drunk man who came in clutching a bottle was turned out at once, for no alcohol was allowed on the premises, as a notice on the wall proclaimed. Other notices about meal times, church services and the football team were stuck here and there, and a budgerigar twittered in a cage on a shelf. I took a bundle of bedding, was told my ward, floor and bed number and set off alone.

It was a rather grim place, for the lift was not in use, and its black iron cage seemed to dominate the stairway. Bits of cigarette packets and other litter lay scattered about, for the place was very understaffed and was cleaned floor by floor during the course of the week. None of the occupants made any attempt to help, for no duties were expected of you beyond making your own bed. Amid the gloom, wall tiles of swirling blue lilies, a relic of the Nineties, struck an aesthetic note. At last I reached the third floor, walked along a dark corridor and into my ward. Old hospital names for the wards were still painted on the walls. One was 'Edinburgh', the Scottish connection again. Seeing the place now, however, any hygiene-minded matron would have a fit.

On entering the ward, and walking across it to find my bed at the far end, I seemed to step into a half-forgotten story of demoralised mercenary soldiers during a civil war, whether in barracks or hospital I could not say. In the half light, for many of the bulbs were missing, I could see rows of beds, each with a man in or on it, and with pin-up pictures and heaps of clothes nearby. Many of the beds were quaintly old-fashioned, made of dark wood, with bow-shaped barred bedsteads. The men were of all ages, from twenty to seventy, mostly unkempt and cross-looking, with no student types, only would-be workmen. Some of them, I later found, did go to work, even doing night shifts in hard manual jobs, yet somehow lacked the drive to find more private accommodation. Great pillars blocked my view of the ward, and somewhere central heating must have been working. Near my bed was a room once used for severely ill patients, with sagging wooden doors held together by a padlock. Through the crack, I could see it was furnished in a makeshift fashion, with orange-box cupboards and socks hanging on a line – also a big alarm clock. Such rooms, hardly ever vacant, cost a few pounds more.

A rather shallow-looking young man watched me unpack, while a ferocious unshaven one in bed stared at me with wolfish intensity. The latter unnerved me considerably for the first two days, until I discovered that he looked at everyone like that, and was simply staring into space. His friend came over and asked if I had a spare button. I gave him one, and he looked at it dubiously and said that he supposed it would have to do. Nearby I found a washroom with extremely hot water and a mirror, and with puddles everywhere. Notices advising nurses how to clean bedpans were still fixed to the wall. I put my odds and ends in the locker by my bed, keeping my pride and joy, a battery razor, in my pocket. Such a razor would be like gold to a down-and-out, and to let anyone see it would have been unspeakable folly.

I sat on the bed and pondered. Each floor had four wards and each ward was full of occupied beds, so the amount of men accommodated was prodigious. All the same, London was still full of down-and-outs, mostly in an alcoholic haze, who slept out of doors. Perhaps the hostel was known in Glasgow, so that sons of the Clyde, adrift in London, were the first to reach its harbour.

By now its was five o'clock and I went downstairs for the evening meal, which was in the basement, next to the kitchen. A queue had already formed. Some of the kitchen staff, I was told, had arrived as inmates and been taken on as staff. They were jovial enough in a rough galley-cook kind of way.

To my chagrin, I could have no tea, as you had to provide your own cup. However, the scullery cat made up for this disappointment, for it had four enchanting kittens, that made even the most hardened vagrant turn sentimental.

I carried my plates into one of the two dining rooms where silent weary-eyed men sat at wooden tables, plying plastic cutlery. The food was good, although with a few hairs, and the salt was piled upon a plate and you helped yourself with finger and thumb. Morning and evening, the basement was neon lit, with few windows, and this gave it a bleak timeless feeling of an old-fashioned all night station waiting room. 'Timeless' cannot be the right word, as after a while I felt as if it was four in the morning and always had been. Conversation consisted of curses and insults, and I found few congenial companions there, the free tramps outside being far more lively-looking. However, that first night I met a gentle old man from South Uist, with a white walrus moustache. He despised the others and was optimistically looking for work, although in his sixty-sixth year.

'Whisky is the enemy of man,' he told me gravely. 'I wasted my whole life as an alcoholic, but now I've cured myself. My sisters are nurses and they won't talk to me.'

I looked around the room, seeing mostly Scots and Englishmen, with one fat Welshman, the butt of many jokes. With full stomachs came a more genial atmosphere. A young queer with a shaven head and piercing eyes wandered in, saluted, cried 'Gay, gay!' and left. He was always doing that, it appeared, and could say nothing else. Finishing my meal, I sauntered out into the Strand, with a feeling of relief, noticing that just across the way, as if in allegory, stood the doom-haunted shuttered-up building of Rhodesia House.

That night, when I returned late, for the door was always open, I thought 'I bet that someone's stolen my things from out of my locker.'

When I got in, I found that not only had they stolen my things, but they'd stolen my *locker*! A clean white space against the wall marked where it had been.

'Take more care in future,' was all the men at the desk said. Next evening I went up to bed quite blithely, edging past two staggering men who were singing 'My Ain Folk' in rich tenor voices. I made for my bed with the confidence of someone who has nothing left to steal. Alas, someone had stolen my bed clothes! Wearily, and with many a warning, the desk-man gave me some more. After that I was not troubled again, and I took my clothes and money under the blankets with me. My bed was very comfortable, although the night was full of shouts and oaths. Perpetual cursing and snarling, I found, was the technique by which they warned one another off from stealing. Nearly everyone there lay . on their bed all day, and I was the only one who went out and explored London. Some of them had long memories of sleepless nights on the Embankment, and only wanted to stay in bed forever.

I would rise at six-thirty and step out onto the balcony, overlooking the Strand. Here I would stand on the soggy easy chair that someone had left there, and gaze out on beautiful and intriguing rooftops and on the street below. No one else used this balcony, and I had a unique view of a busy corner of London. Sometimes I would pretend to be a blend of king, dictator and mad prophet, addressing an imaginary crowd below, hundreds of moon faces, oafish collectivised peasants, staring up at me.

'My people, I speak to you not in sorrow, but in anger! Go, my people, and drown your unworthy selves in the Thames.'

Sadly they would turn around and shuffle off to perform this task, with heads bowed, and I would go down to breakfast feeling much refreshed. Then out, out into the magic city of London!

At the Embankment coffee stall, the same rogues gathered as of yore, boasting of petty crimes and of places they had found to sleep. I would shave in an out-of-order photo booth, and then follow the Thames either towards the West or the East End. Slowly a glow of light would illuminate the river as the sun rose, and the water seemed to flow past in separate islands of ripple, all linked like the plumes in a peacock's tail. This comparison pleased me, until to my mortification I found that Kipling, who once lived nearby, had used it first to describe an Indian river. Mud banks on the Thames have a strange appearance to me, the only part of London that hasn't changed since the Romans were here, since, after all, mud is mud. Lesser black backed gulls and other birds made arrow footprints on this historic mud.

Spendthrift's London is a wonderful place, and later in the day I would roam into Soho and see, just behind the Windmill Theatre, among all the strip clubs, innocence in the form of happy little Chinese children, beautifully dressed, hurrying into St James's and St Peter's Church of England Primary School. Chinese families are almost the only residents in the district, and a notice outside the school was in Chinese. Lessons must have been in English, as few, if any, of the teachers came from China. After the squalor of St Mungo's it was pleasant also to walk in Trafalgar Square and see fresh-faced provincial families up for a day's treat, feeding the pigeons.

On Sunday morning I walked into the East End, arriving in time to worship at St Paul's Church in Dock Street, a church for seamen, though few attend. They have a hostel of their own next door, and need not disturb St Mungo. A friendly church, St Paul's was built in 1849 and has a weathercock in the form of a ship in full sail. A little primary school, attached to the church, stands nearby, also with a ship on top. It looks like a village school.

Later, in the Whitechapel Art Gallery, I disgraced myself by trying to shave with the battery razor in this hallowed abode of trendiness. A bohemian young man stopped me at once, although I begged him to look on me as a living work of art, possibly for sale to a wealthy female patron. Banished, I crossed the road and sat on a log in the park and began to buzz away.

A shabby mob of tramps stared at me greedily, their eyes lighting up with the strange unearthly glow of a tramp who sees an electric razor. Finally they sent across an emissary in the shape of a ragged young midget girl with a large but cheerful head.

'Can my friends borrow your razor?' she asked.

'Well, no, as I'm using it, you see,' I replied, switching off. In perfect good humour she tried to wrest it from my grasp, but after a moment's struggle I broke free and ran.

'Oh blast!' I heard her cry in resignation as I reached the gate and safety. Pity we had to meet that way, as in happier circumstances I would have liked to have got to know her.

In the doorway of the Whitechapel library, which I visited next day, I admired the picture, painted on glazed tiles, of the East End in the eighteenth century. It showed smocked farm labourers driving haycarts through the streets, to the ribald wonder of the dandyish young City apprentices. This picture, the work of a forgotten Victorian artist, had been removed from a demolished pub. Fittingly enough, it has been copied recently by another East End pub artist, at The Cart and Horses, Stratford East. There the same figures, in garish colours, appear on the pub's outside wall, to an incongruous background of Alpine scenery.

Crossing the road by the tube station, I made for one of my old haunts, Cable Street. Many years ago, in the Sixties, I had a room just off Cable Street, and at night I would find myself in a lesser-known Soho whose 'vice barons' were African immigrants. Now the clubs where so many human dramas and tragedies were acted nightly have been swept away. Respectable flats have covered the sites of cobbled alleys and tumbledown cottages, and at first glance Cable Street might now seem to be as mundane as any other council neighbourhood. Immigrants have moved elsewhere, and the Street has a new English atmosphere which I now set out to explore.

One thing I did *not* expect to see was a good secondhand bookshop, but there it was, on the corner of Dock Street – 'The Cheapest Bookshop in the World'. Nor was this an idle boast, although the books were well thumbed, as they had all belonged to ships' libraries and bore the imprint of the Marine Society, a ferocious-looking sea dog with a scaly tail, holding a torch of knowledge as if it were Neptune's trident. Also for sale were small wooden sea chests that had once held books, and would now make good children's play boxes, especially if painted in bright colours. I had never dreamed sailors were such a bookish lot.

Going on my way, I soon came to a row of distinguished, if soot-blackened, Georgian houses, one of which was used as a school. The playground nearby, a rather dismal place when empty, was enlivened by an attractive mural on the wall, for once *not* in the splodgy mock-children's-art style usually used in playgrounds.

A few yards further on, and I came to *the* mural. This is to commemorate the Battle of Cable Street, and was then being painted on the side of the town hall, a large white building. A stocky, bearded man, the artist, who seemed quite at home on ladder and scaffolding, told me that he would not be finished for three years. Displayed on a notice board nearby, the complete mural design showed a swirling sketchily painted maelstrom of East Enders attacking policemen wherever they found them. One mounted rozzer struck blindly at the victorious People with his swagger stick, another, with his wild-eyed horse, came crashing to the ground. A woman leaning from a window emptied a chamber pot over a policeman's head. What effect could such a mural have in a rough neighbourhood, both on the children and others called on to admire it, and on a young policeman setting out for the first time on a difficult beat?

Apparently, the real 'battle', in the far off Thirties, happened like this. Two groups of outsiders, the Blackshirts and the Communists, converged on Cable Street and marched straight at one another with the evident intention of fighting to the death. Blackshirts chose the East End to march in so as to intimidate the Jews who lived there. In the same way, the National Front marches in Lewisham nowadays because of the West Indians who live there, but fights other groups of outsiders, the Socialist Workers' Party and the Anti-Nazi League. In Cable Street, residents watched in horror or annoyance as mad marchers prepared for war. One side was chanting 'We gotta get rid of the Yids' and the other, no less deluded, was declaring 'They Shall Not Pass', a slogan borrowed from the Spanish Civil War. It sounds better in

Spanish. London's long-suffering police, some on horseback, managed with a great deal of trouble to send the hooligans packing.

However, the myth of the Battle of Cable Street, one in which the artist passionately believed, is that of a fight between the People and the Police, the latter helped by ranks of Blackshirts, but defeated none the less. Instead of middle-class Communists and hired toughs from all over London, the 'shall not passers' of the myth were ordinary East Enders, who successfully resisted Fascism in its twin forms of Black-shirts and Blue Helmets.

However the muralist was not to have everything his own way. Not long after my visit, 'right-wing vandals' defaced the huge painting with anti-Communist slogans in huge brown letters, using a virulent form of indelible paint, impossible to scrub out and hard to paint over.

In a rage, the muralist resigned, and a new man took on the job. Today's complete mural, a totally different and far better picture, in my estimation, shows a more realistic 'battle' in rich lustrous colours. It is worth going to Cable Street to see it.

Near the mural is the entrance to the churchyard of St George-in-the-East, which overlooks a Methodist mission for down-and-out men. I could see what appeared to be a soup kitchen, with vociferous Irish-looking tramps lurching in and out, from the semi-derelict church grounds where I had been trying to read eighteenth-century dates on tombstones. The church itself, a vast white building that towers over Cable Street, is of a later period and seemed disused on my visit. A window-shattered ruined hut in the churchyard bears the legend, in archaic lettering, of 'Nature Study Museum'.

Deciding to study human nature instead, I joined the tramps. It turned out I was in a tea kitchen, not a soup one, and as I helped myself to a buckshee cup from the urn, I reflected that I should come there more often. Ugly but genial broken men sat around the tables, some arguing with Hogarthian gestures, others staring blankly, and a few quietly trying to sleep. Someone, perhaps a former fish porter, had written this poem on one table, using a felt-tip:

'You can wash it with soap,

You can scrub it with soda,
But you'll never get rid of
That Billingsgate odour.'

Tramps never seem to volunteer to clean the premises that Charity provides for them, but these ones at least pulled their legs and chairs in as patient young Methodists swept and cleaned around them.

I finished my tea and left, and soon reached the end of Cable Street and joined Commercial Road. This busy thoroughfare has some quaint and remarkable sidestreets leading from it. Those approaching the London Hospital, terraces strange and grim, resemble old photographs of the East End with the children, rabbis and cloth-capped loungers removed. Close by are flats built by nineteenth-century philanthropists, in a bizarre style once common in London. Sunken, almost tunnel-like, recreation yards divide these red-brick buildings, with their slate roofs, dormer windows and dark stone-stepped interiors. Each row, and each yard, is a street in length, and grumpy but very law-abiding Indians stump uncomprehendingly past brickwork painted with 'Anarchy Now' slogans. Their gentle dark-eyed children play on the pavements or run errands gladly. The East End is a place much visited by radicals, a theatre of revolution whose play-actors live elsewhere.

Further East, towards Stepney Green, many old houses have been smartened up and look most attractive. 'Gentrification', if it comes, should help to keep the demolition men at bay.

While musing and wandering around these backstreets, away from Commercial Road, I came suddenly upon Stepney churchyard, a place I had never seen before. A park in itself, with tree-lined walks, it has a children's playground in full song, rows of girls and boys chanting out street ditties of the East End as they swing merrily to and fro:

'My name is Elvis Presley,
Girls are sexy,
Sitting in the Roxy,
Drinking Pepsi.
O–U–T spells out!'

After chanting this five times, as if it were the five times table in the schools of my childhood, the songsters changed to 'My boyfriend bought me apples, my boyfriend bought me pears', and their shrill voices followed me as I walked down to the church of St Dunstan and All Saints. A mellow grey stone building, the church has stood since Saxon times, but was now locked. The oldest tombstone I could find was dated 1816, as against 1767 at St George-in-the-East.

Turning away from the church, I stared in amazement at a small flock of sheep quietly grazing on the other side of the road. Hurrying over, I found myself at Stepping Stone Farm, a community-run venture, with something of the air of a playgroup and pets' corner about it, and a contented collection of sheep, goats, horses and poultry ambling around its spacious paddocks. Even though some of the determined-looking girls in charge may have waffled on about environmental ecology if asked, the farm made a delightful oasis in mid-London, and pleased the local children almost as much as the swings across the road. It was one of ten City Farms, I was told.

With many confusing directions, the City Farmers pointed me towards Whitechapel, where I took the Cambridge Heath Road to Bethnal Green and soon was sitting comfortably in the back kitchen of Charlie's Café, whose owner is a friend of mine, eating enormous quantities of the hot bacon sandwiches for which that establishment is so justly renowned.

Roaming round the East End on other occasions, I found many hostels for men, all very gloomy looking; and even, in Brune Street, a Soup Kitchen for the Jewish Poor. This title was engraved in stone, looking very picturesque, and dated 1902. To my astonishment, it was still 'fully operational', as they say, and as there is Jewish blood in my family, I wondered if I was entitled to half a cup. Inside I found a row of little gnome-like people sitting on a waiting room bench, and one of them told me I would have to go to Beaumont Square for a letter of recommendation, after which I would be given a ticket. This I was reluctant to do, so I left and headed back to Whitechapel, passing boarded-up council flats with Indians living in the few that were still in use.

On my way, a young Irishman demanded alms, blocking my path in great excitement, but I shook him off and ran down Fournier Street into busy Brick Lane.

After this, it was good to head back for the Strand, and to soothe my nerves beneath the noble plane trees of Lincoln's Inn. There I found a library for those reading for the bar, a gem of carved wood and stained glass, almost like a City church, although most of the scholars were Hindus. Next day, Canon Gundry, the *Daily Telegraph* church correspondent, took me to the Athenaeum. It felt rather bizarre to leave the oak panels, busts and marble columns for St Mungo's once more. Fortunately my tattered conformist's sports jacket served equally well as dress for a tramp or a clubman.

Knowing the club only from Disraeli novels, which omitted detail, I blotted my copy book once again by waiting for coffee in the dining room, whereas it was served in a kind of Long Chamber upstairs. There I was most intrigued by a silver mounted ram's horn full of snuff.

Everyone I met at the *Daily Telegraph* offices was extremely kind and attentive to me. I don't know where the myth of journalism as a 'dog eat dog' profession comes from. I was asked to contribute to various columns, and later on, to write book reviews for the sister paper, the *Sunday Telegraph*. My trip to London had proved a fruitful one indeed.

So at last my visit to St Mungo's drew to an end, and as always, I met the most interesting characters just as I was leaving. One of these was an elderly man who walked from the hostel to Barking and back, almost every evening, for the exercise. He had a day-time job, and said that if he could ever find a room for twenty pounds a week, he would be thankful to leave St Mungo's. There were even a couple of literary men, one of whom had written an unpublished book on chess. The other supplied bottom-of-the-page jokes to *Readers' Digest*. Their conversation was a curious mixture of cultured accents and Embankment slang.

'I find myself a bit "under the arm", today, old chap, so I was wondering . . .'

'I'm a trifly boracic myself, or I'd be delighted to oblige.'

('Boracic' equals 'boracic lint' equals 'skint'.)

From the surrounding tables the conversation was more predictable.

'So I stole this bottle and sold it.'

'This guy asked me to stay at his house, but I said "no". He wasn't a queer or anything, but he might have cut my throat.'

'Scabby headed Welsh git!'

One of the young Glaswegians, with a very bawdy repertoire of anecdotes, was different from everyone else in that he was uproariously cheerful the whole time, with an enormous grin. For some reason he always wore an American 'deer hunter's' cap with flaps over his ears. Another happy man, his moods flashing to anger and back again within seconds, was a little tough brown person with an enormous pillar box smile.

'Are you a Gurkha?' I asked him.

'Why?' he asked quickly, reaching as if for his kukri blade.

'I've always wanted to meet a Gurkha,' I replied. 'How do you do?'

'Ha!' he replied, pleased. 'If this was a war, I would throw a pinch of sand in your eyes, so! and then cut off your head.'

Satisfied that he had ingratiated himself by this remark, he sat down to his meal.

A strange dreamy-eyed plump young man with a very soft voice, an unshaven round face and a cloth cap, was known as 'the Pearly', because his many badges and expensive lion's head buckled belt made him resemble a dressed-up costermonger.

On my last night at the hostel, lying in bed, I heard an unpleasant upper-class queer's voice ringing out from the pitch blackness, urging someone not to be so silly and adding that he had sent out for a bottle.

'Boo hoo! Boo hoo!' the someone cried, actually making that sound.

A fight then took place, was drawn, and then I fell asleep. As I had just read *The Ordeal of Gilbert Pinfold*, I wondered if I wasn't just hearing things, like the hero of that book.

So it was a relief in the morning when I heard the fight being described by several people to the Pearly. He had been the one who was crying, and who had struck the first blow, but as he was sozzled at the time, he couldn't remember a thing, and listened in wonder, looking on the whole episode as a tribute to the good time he must have had.

That was the morning I left St Mungo's, to everyone's amazement, for no one left as a rule; the Legion of the Damned.

'Why are you leaving us? Have you any problems?' asked a most concerned man at the desk.

They, the staff, were the ones with problems, as I never counted more than ten of them, as opposed to hundreds of inmates. I never enquired into the administration, but I gathered it was a private charity founded by a Glaswegian who felt sorry for down-and-out Scots. Looking after such people is a thankless task, as they seldom say 'thank you' and tend to grow in resentment to the proportion that they are helped. Ideally, the staff should have included fifty more cleaners and an orderly, or a tough matron, on permanent duty in each of the wards. Volunteers step forward!

Outside, I told a passing tramp that a bed was now vacant. He was another cheery soul, despite the fact that he had a festering red sore where his right eye should have been.

'St Mungo's? No, I'd never go there!' he shouted.

I hope the saint was not hurt, for the man was an Irishman, and so perhaps not a part of his ministry.

During my stay at St Mungo's, I had made full use of the lunch vouchers kindly supplied by the Hare Krishna people. Before going home, I went off on an adventure with them, which I shall describe in the next chapter.

[PART FIVE]
Hare Krishna

One day, when hungry, I found my way to the Hare Krishna temple near Soho Square, as I had a free ticket for a vegetarian meal there. To my delight, I found a most expensive restaurant at the address given, full of smart professional-looking young people eating salad. Wandering around, holding my ticket, I at last found a group of young Hare Krishna men, with shaved heads and pony tails, the sort of people you see dancing down Oxford Street. They seemed incredulous at my mistake, and at once sent me packing to another door outside.

Narrow steps led up to the temple, which was above the cult-owned restaurant. A small crowd had already arrived in the hall, and I gave my ticket to a Krishna-ite who sat on the stairs. He asked me to take my shoes off, which I did. In time-honoured Mission tradition, we were expected to listen to 'religion' before eating, and I was more than happy to do this. A plump middle-aged man with glasses and a shaven head rose from a desk and opened the temple door. From his air of kindly, if harassed authority, I named him 'the Abbot'.

It was a brilliant, gaudy temple. Entering it felt like stepping inside an old music box, newly polished, or perhaps into a toy theatre set for an Oriental extravaganza. A slithery polished floor gave it an English touch, as in India you would expect age-old stone flags to sit on. Here they provided cushions. Although nearly all the Hare Krishnas were English, many of them from Lancashire, they prided themselves on being more Indian than the Indians, as I was to discover. The temple was supposedly built to plans supplied in the Vedic scriptures, two thousand years before Christ, and gallons of gold paint must have been used. Columns and window and door frames had been given an ornate Ali Baba treatment, and scenes from the life of Krishna decorated the walls. There was also a chart for devotees, who were encouraged to bring in twenty-one pounds a day for Krishna. We all sat facing a curtained stage, or altar, with chairs in front of it and framed portraits resting on them, garlanded with flowers. These showed a peevish bald Indian with spectacles. He looked distinctly dry and academic, and I didn't know what they saw in him. Also scattered about were microphones, tape recorders, harmoniums, sitars and Indian drums, the sort you hang around your neck and beat on each end. Mysterious slippers were placed before each picture. A pink-cheeked English girl in a sari padded in and switched on a tape recorder, which broke into discordant music.

Quickly, the temple filled up. As well as myself, there were a few Continental students, an earnest Indian, probably a law student, a rough tattooed young man with small eyes and short hair, who looked distinctly menacing, two unkempt hippie types, very down and out, a complete Persian family with enchanting children, an intense soulful girl whose Irish peasant features were heightened by her head scarf, and two bright-looking schoolboys of fifteen or so, who clutched a long-playing record sold to them by a Hare Krishna. With the company, but not of it, was a very old, infirm-looking tramp, who sat on a chair, not on the floor, and seemed highly indignant at having to support heathenism in order to support himself. He was one of the hungry few, who depended on Krishna for his lunch.

A tall pleasant-faced young man in the usual pale orange robes and top-knot stepped into the room and addressed us through the microphone in a slight American accent. Nevertheless he came from Herefordshire, but the style of most new religions is as American as it is Oriental. As with rock-and-roll, perhaps transatlantic tones are obligatory. In India, orange is the traditional colour for holy men's robes.

I must say, his speech was fairly sensible. He ran down scientists for their material approach to life, as if people were machines fuelled by food and drink, and requiring only to be kept warm, dry and in good running order. Then he praised the soul. Everyone was drinking it in, and rightly so, as nothing is more pleasing than to hear our inner conviction of immortality voiced openly by someone in authority. I wonder that more vicars don't try it. The purest, most moving testimony to God I have ever heard had come from a young girl who concluded her heartfelt speech by worshipping an image of the Guru Maharaji, whose disciples had told her that she had a soul. Infant school lessons, forgotten in cynical secondary school, are nowadays rediscovered in strange forms.

However, the young man, in speaking of present-day materialism, seemed to think that the government, the advertisers, pornographers and scientists, were all one and the same body, in league with one another to enslave the nation. He didn't seem to think there could be any diversity of opinion in the 'material world', or world of non-Hare Krishnas. I was later to be told that the Church of England was 'bogus, as it was started by Henry the Fifth' and to read criticisms of scientists, which though well founded, were put in the crude terms of Soviet propaganda – 'these rascals must be kicked out', possibly into the dustbin of history. Notions of the soul, the divine and the immortal were presented as being the patented inventions of the Hare Krishna movement.

It is often the element of truth in strange cults that attracts young people, as much as the dressing up and the joys of belonging to a secret society. Believing that they are the sole possessors of the truth is also a great attraction. No hypnotising or brainwashing are necessary, for once you are in a cult of your choosing, you are simply never allowed to have time to think, or to make proper contact with those outside.

Anyway, the young man's talk made quite an impact on the crowd, the tramp apart, and he then asked if there were any questions. The Irish peasant girl, quite entranced, went on her knees and bowed, for she was already a devotee. So, to my surprise was the ruffianly tattooed young man, and one of the hippies, for they lay prostrate before the altar, eyes closed in evident bliss. The Persians, also, were believers, and the schoolboys, eyes shining, seemed disposed to believe everything they heard.

'Why do you shave your heads?' asked the other hippie, whose hair was very long.

'Well, we associate long hair with vanity, and prefer not to have any, to avoid being tempted to pride.'

There must have been more to it than that, or why did they keep a tuft, or scalp lock, at the back?

'Are you Hindus?' I asked, putting my hand up.

'No, we come from the dawn of history, long before Hindus, and base our belief on the original Vedic scriptures. Hindus later partially followed the same scriptures.'

This wouldn't do and the intense Indian scrambled to his feet, spectacles flashing, as he defended his faith.

'I am a Hindu,' he cried, looking deeply hurt 'and I say, it is *you* who have borrowed from *us*! The Vedic scriptures are the Hindu writings, very ancient. No one had heard of you people until a few years ago. How can you say that you come from before Hindus?'

He went on, very learnedly, at some length, and the man from Herefordshire with the Californian twang could only repeat that he went by the Vedic scriptures and the Hindus did not. At length, the dismayed Hindu sat down.

I was later to learn that the man in the photograph was his Divine Grace A. C. Bhaktidevanta, who founded the movement in 1976, and who died in 'seventy-seven, chanting 'Hare Krishna' to the last, under anaesthetic. Revered as near-god and totalitarian leader, his name is significant, for the Bhakti, or devotional branch of Hinduism, seems to have been his inspiration. A reaction against over-intellectualism, the Bhakti movement began to flourish in our later Middle Ages, with Krishna as its central figure, and with no emphasis on caste. Perhaps Bhakti itself is too intellectual for modern Britain, and the Hare Krishna movement is a partly simplified, partly exaggerated break-away version of it. Certainly one of the Hare Krishna devotees I met was newly named Yamenacarya, after a Bhakti philosopher. All the devotees had new names, by the way, and one girl I met said that she was called Aruna, or Reddish Eyed – scarcely a compliment!

Do not suppose that I know what I'm talking about – much of this information I obtained later from the Hindu, who seemed overjoyed that I took him seriously.

The Hindu disposed of for the moment, I played the pest myself, and put up my hand once more.

'Is that a picture of Krishna on the wall?' I asked pointing.

'Yes,' came the admission, and this caused rather a stir, as the picture in question was of a man with a lion's head, its fangs bared fiendishly as it ripped the body of a young girl apart, blood spurting out in plenty.

'Why is he being so horrible to that poor girl?'

'He is doing her a favour, by liberating her from her earthly body.'

'I hope no one liberates *me* that way. You might as well worship a murderer.'

'No, she is glad to be set free by Krishna, but she'd run away from a murderer.'

'Well, I'd run a lot faster from a man with a lion's head myself.'

This got me some cheap laughs from the schoolboys. As far as I can make out, the same Eastern gods have kindly and terrifying Aspects, as if Satan were admitted to the Trinity (awful thought)! Celtic paganism, itself somewhat Indian, used the same idea, and we still have good St Nicholas and wretched Old Nick.

'At this point we usually introduce a little music and chanting,' the young man said smilingly. A chart was hung over the curtains, with the Hare Krishna mantra written out in full on it, and other young men slipped in through a side door and picked up the musical instruments. Through a chink in the curtain I could see the pink girl waving a white plume. Then she tinkled some bells, blew into a conch, and the show was on the road. First of all the harmonium, played awkwardly by a robed young man sitting cross legged on the floor, put me in mind of a Sunday School in some grim industrial town. However, cymbals and drum added an Eastern rhythm, and soon we were all chanting and rocking about on our cushions, led on by the Herefordshire lad.

'Hare Krishna, Hare Krishna, Krishna Krishna, Hare Hare!
Hare Rama, Hare Rama, Rama Rama, Hare Hare!'

('Hare' was pronounced 'Harry')

Faster and faster the rhythm went, the drum player went beserk and jigged about the room, and the harmonium man grew frenetic. We were encouraged to dance, and nearly everyone performed a sort of conga, while I played 'Here we go round the Mulberry Bush' with the Persian children. Everyone was having a good time, and chanting faster and faster.

'Hurry up food, hurry up food, hurry hurry!' I sang, knowing that no one could hear me.

Suddenly it all ended, and we were allowed to go upstairs for our meal. I stayed behind for a few minutes to be shown how to chant on the beads, which you work round and round in your hand, never touching the great Krishna bead. Then I too went upstairs.

Low tables and cushions were arranged around a long room, and devotees were ladling out portions of rice and vegetables into stainless steel bowls. As we ate, the devotees came and spoke to us. On my right sat a woman and her daughter, whom I had not noticed before. Both were eager to join the movement, and the girl had been taken all the way from a convent school in Liverpool to attend. On my left was the hippie who had asked about the hair, and a cross-legged devotee was talking to him.

'Yeh, I'm stayin' in the Sally Ann hostel, but it's really heavy,' the hippie said. 'All these old dossers, an' it costs quite a bit, an' the dossers keep stealing my fings and that, all sleepin' in rows together.'

'Come to the Manor!' urged the devotee. 'That's our retreat – Bhaktidevanta Manor in Hertfordshire. You'd love it there! Be a weekend guest – we'll give you a sleeping bag!'

'Yeh, well, I dunno what you'll do to me,' he replied.

'I'll go!' I chimed in, always ready for a country-house weekend. 'When do we leave?'

This disconcerted the devotee, who pointed out someone else to ask. At the end of the room, washing-up preparations were being made, and one top-knot man was snapping at another, who seemed quite upset. On my way over to them, I passed the schoolboys, who were holding the record and chattering happily to the Abbot about the famous rock stars who had played on it to glorify Krishna. I knew all about that record, as long ago I had been approached by a tall man looking very thug-like in a Balaclava helmet, put on to disguise his scalp lock, so no one could tell he was a Hare Krishna. However I had already overheard two other Balaclava men discussing Krishna, so I was forewarned.

'Do you want a free record?' the man had asked me. 'Just give whatever you like to charity.'

'What charity?' I enquired.

'A charity that helps young people in trouble.'

'That seems reasonable,' I said and took the record. 'Let's see now – here you are.' And I handed him twopence and started to walk away. Violently, he snatched the record back.

'You've got to give at least three pounds,' he told me sternly, but he did give me back my twopence.

I think I got off lightly, as not having a rock record is a treat in itself. The schoolboys, however, thought otherwise, and were very pleased, although they knew the 'charity' was only Hare Krishna.

I found the devotee who knew about trips to the Manor, and after looking at me suspiciously, he ordered me to do the washing up. This was partly to test how keen I was, and partly to get the washing up done. He gargled and spat in the sink over the dishes.

'Some of the devotees could give you a lift when they've finished working in the restaurant,' he told me.

My co-washer up was the other hippie, the religious one. He turned out to be a half-wit who could barely speak.

'I swear that guy – that guy at the Manor – I swear, he was real, you know! I looked at him and he was real!' he blurted out, with difficulty.

'He means the wax image in the Temple there,' I heard someone say.

After seeing my attempts at washing up, the devotee dismissed me and I went downstairs, borrowed a Krishna magazine and sat and read it in the temple. To my delight, the curtain was now pulled back, to reveal a tableau with large pale blue Indian dolls. With the help of the magazine, which had beautiful pictures of blue boy Krishna leading the white calves along, a popular Indian legend, I identified the dolls as 'Flute playing Lord Krishna and His eternal consort Srimati Radharami'.

Then I noticed the Irish girl, stretched flat on the floor, face downwards. After a moment she arose and began to walk rapidly around the temple, muttering the 'Hare Krishna' rigmarole over and over again as if in anguish. She looked right through me with her wide haunted tragic eyes, her transparent headscarf now giving her an eerie phantom quality. Friends who know India tell me that mantra chanting can lead to beautiful visions of the gods, but this poor girl seemed to be looking at a terrifying vision of Kali.

After a while I came out and enquired about my shoes. Someone went to fetch them, while I chatted with the Abbot, who told me of an heroic Hare Krishna he knew who chanted for twenty-four hours without stopping. Just then the devotee who had promised me a lift came downstairs.

'Ah, this man said I could go to the Manor,' I told the Abbot.

'Did *I* say that?' the man replied, in icy dangerous tones. 'Think carefully – did *I* say that? I merely said I would enquire about it.'

'Don't worry, I'm sure you can go,' said the Abbot reassuringly.

For several days after that I attended meetings and ate vegetarian meals and allowed girl devotees in the street to stick black smiling Krishna badges on me. 'Krishna' originally meant 'black', I believe.

Finally I gained their confidence, and we sat, four in a van, bowling up to the Manor in Hertfordshire. North through Camden Town we sped, and somewhere past Swiss Cottage I saw a man in vest and pants bobbing up and down in a glass fronted hotel lounge. He appeared to be on a stationary bicycle.

'Look at that!' said the devotee who was driving. 'That's pure material world!'

'Whatever is he doing?' I asked.

'He's slimming, in order to have sex. That's all the material world thinks about – sex.'

Privately, I thought that the man might just be slimming in order to be slim, but I said nothing. Soon we were on a ghastly orange-lit concrete road, and my companions began to talk nostalgically of India, where they had all been.

'There was this pool for swimming, but you had to look out for snakes and turtles. They told me the pool was four elephants deep.'

This standard of measurement appealed to me, and seeing my look of approval, the devotee asked me if I would like to work for Krishna. I doubted if I was worthy, and they didn't press the point. Before long we had left the main road, and were driving into the village of Letchmore Heath where the Manor was.

Noticing a dog sniffing about on the verge, the driver said 'And they say dogs haven't got souls!' in a tone of deep scorn.

Again I approved, as I had not yet realised that they regarded dogs as a punishment for wayward souls whose time had come for reincarnation.

In the stable yard of Bhaktidevanta Manor we all scrambled out and went inside. It was a sprawling half-timbered building which they swore was Elizabethan, but which looked to me more like Weybridge Tudor. Very much a pop star's choice of mansion, and in fact it was given to the Krishnas by George Harrison, the former Beatle.

'We've got a new mansion near Worcester now,' the driver told me. 'It's a massive place, which we bought off the Earl of Coventry, and we're starting a school for the children there.'

Poor little mites! Did the Fabians who plotted the downfall of the country houses they themselves lived in, ever foresee *this* use for so many of them? How quickly an Age of Reason leads to an Age of Unreason!

Inside, I took my shoes off and put them in a cubby hole provided, and was led past a tiny room marked 'Krsna's Kitchen – Private' into a large hall. 'Krsna' meant the same as 'Krishna', I suppose.

Glass windows opened out to the Temple, probably the former ballroom, with a polished wooden floor and a stage at each end.

'You're in luck, as one of the eleven perfect spiritual masters is here at the moment,' I was told.

Dancing of enormous fervour was taking place, and the Temple presented an extraordinary sight. All the men wore robes and had shaven heads with a streak of white paint on the forehead. Drums, conches and cymbals kept up a cacophonous racket, faster and faster, and the men leaped up and down on the spot, arms above their heads. It reminded me rather of a disco. Nearby, always separate from the men, the women in saris swayed, clapped and wailed in an Eastern tongue. The same picture of Krishna as a lion dismembering one of them hung on the wall here, much enlarged. All the devotees were young, but the girls particularly so, some seeming no more than seventeen. Others had small children or babies with them. Shaven heads made the men indistinguishable to me, and the girls, who were allowed hair, looked much more individualistic, though very serious and impassioned. Hop, hop went the men! Sway, sway went the women! Chanting and wailing alternated and little stampedes often took place, as the music crashed on relentlessly. A male devotee handed out flowers and another had a purifying flame. You were supposed to whisk your hand through this, and then pass it over your head. At one end of the room a grinning black golliwog mask peered from a gilded shrine covered in flowers. This was Krishna in the form of Jaganatha, Lord of the Universe, who rides in a juggernaut. The other end of the room had two thrones, one on a pedestal containing a life size waxwork of a grim looking bald Indian – could this be another god, or the deceased Founder? Anyway, this must have been the figure which the hippie had thought was 'real'.

Incense smothered the air, cymbals battered my senses and yet the wild leaping and praying showed no sign of ceasing. Talk about High Church! Sometimes everyone went on their knees, the men bowing so deeply that their heads were completely upside down and their pony-tails dangling. One or two real Indians were among them. Suddenly a door was opened, and with great excitement a red carpet was rolled out in the next room. Processions of men began to leap along this carpet, greeted rapturously by the girls, who were now also waving their arms in the air. Mullioned windows were opened to the night, and young men rushed in and out, jigging up and down, no doubt to the consternation of the natives and those who had retired to Letchmore Heath for a quiet life. From outside, framed in the light, these window dancers must have presented a scene as from Hell. Villagers far away must have stirred from their firesides uneasily, hearing drums.

A roar made me look around, and behold, the Perfect Master, incarnate in the flesh, was sitting on the lower throne. Like his predecessor, he was a morose little Indian with glasses and a genuinely bald head. After he had spoken a few words of greeting the devotees raised both arms in an ecstatic salute and roared in unison, again and again, until a political comparison occurred to me. Seeing such adulation, a self-satisfied smile flickered for a moment around his features, and then he relaxed into petty irritation. Everyone sat cross legged and listened to his message.

'In this Age of Kali, we must turn our back on the material world . . .'

By now, I felt faint, from hunger as much as anything else, and the next room being a lounge, I curled up on a settee and half-listened through the open door. A very kind devotee brought me some delicious fruit salad, which I shared with two very polite Indian children, whose pleasant-looking parents wore Western clothes. They must have been guests like myself. Another guest was a young girl with 'Soho' written all over her defiant face, and she too seemed to think she was in a madhouse. Hare Krishna girls with children never seemed to have husbands or boyfriends, and there appeared to be no endearments or contact at all between the sexes.

Sleepily, I heard a devotee talking of 'deedies', which turned out to be 'deities' as spoken in the usual sub-American accent.

'All who don't become Krishna-conscious are like hogs and dogs and cats,' the Master concluded, and as he left, the chanting began.

Everyone worked their beads like mad as they chanted, for they all wore bead bags slung around their necks and kept one hand inside, working round and round. Someone gave me a set of beads, and I woke up and strolled around, noticing that many of the girls sewed or knitted while chanting, very sensibly. They seemed a docile lot.

A visitors' book showed that guests came from all walks of life –

labourers, factory workers, clerks, students and the occasional archi-
tect or barrister. Most of them were Indians, and few can have
remained to pray, as the residents were nearly all English.
Unfortunately, I could not talk to anyone, as the chant was on
everyone's lips going faster and faster, rama ramas rippling out like the
patter of a Kentucky tobacco auctioneer. Although they stopped
politely and answered 'yes' or 'no', when they had to, it seemed a bit
mean to set back their hopes for a good reincarnation by idle gossip.

'Chanting Hare Krishna is the Path to Liberation,' read one of their
booklets. 'If you cannot chant more than sixteen times a day, you are
simply an animal.'

Catholics believe that 'Ave Marias' can free souls from purgatory,
but even the most obsessive would seem backsliders compared to
Krishna-ites. Krishna-chanting had become not only a substitute for
thought and conversation, but almost a hysteria, with only the devotee's
own soul counting for anything. If your soul is your individuality, the
thing that makes you *you*, then they were losing their souls, not finding
them.

My friend with the fruit salad next showed me where I would sleep.
Twisting dirty narrow stairs led up to a corridor with sleeping rooms – I
won't say bedrooms, because there were no beds, only sleeping bags. It
all looked rather squalid. In my room, however, there were also
mattresses fixed to the floor, a washbasin and a wardrobe.

'Take your money out of the pockets, or it might get stolen,' I was
told, as I hung my coat up. 'If you go to the toilet, take your socks off, or
you'll defile the temple when you go back to dance.'

I didn't see the 'Ladies' Asram', or quarters, but their entrance
looked equally spartan. This was ironical, as the administrators' floor
below was polished and grandiose. One room had a plate on the door
reading 'His Divine Grace' and another had a large notice, 'Life
Membership Reception'. What a thought!

'Krishna is hungry,' I heard someone say downstairs, and I followed
the crowd into a bare room that must have looked quite splendid in its
stately home days. Dark oak panels did look extremely old, and there

was a carved stone fireplace and enormous windows, a mass of neo-Gothic panes.

Food was dished out from a long table, but it was a very different quality to that served in Soho. Ugh! It was cold, slimy and nauseating; black specks in the rice and I swear the Brussels sprouts had gone off! Everyone sat on the floor and dabbled their fingers, for eating was done with the right hand in Indian style, and they set to with a will.

Their table manners appalled me, as did their indecent greed, but I later came across a page of their holy writ which said that 'the spiritual master is always offering Krsna four kinds of delicious food (analysed as that which is licked, chewed, drunk and sucked).'

It was the licking which put me off the most, and every paper plate but mine was soon well scoured. We dropped the used plates in a bin, but a shocked devotee rescued my full one and took it back to the kitchen, evidently for recycling.

Nor was I supposed to go out to a pub for crisps, because 'outside food may have been prepared by wicked people and contains caffein.'

This was no place for a coffee-addict like myself! The only drink was water.

More dancing and chanting then took place. Some of the women, evidently in positions of authority, were dressed rather like nuns and nurses in white and grey. The Soho girl had now vanished, unless disguised in a sari. As for the men, though smiling, they seemed featureless and forgettable.

One of them, who seemed to know me, led me up to bed. Dancing and chanting began at four in the morning and we had to be up, dressed and showered before then. On the landing, a cross-legged devotee chanting to himself gave me quite a shock, as he was naked save for a loin cloth, and very pink.

I ignored the instructions on washing ('How to apply Tilaka') over the basin, and soon I was snug in my sleeping bag with my head on a small cushion. A very tall dark Indian, with a spiteful look about him, was the only other guest.

'I'm from South Africa,' he told the sympathetic dormitory prefect.

'Yes Durban, that's right. It's a great place for me to minister, and tell people about Krishna. No, not Negroes or white people, only Indians. If I was to go up to a white man in the street there, he'd slap my face!'

I didn't believe a word of it. The light was very bright, and the prefect put on a loud tape of Krishna chanting. Would my brain be washed, and tapes and lights be kept on all night? Happily, they were switched off, and in a moment I was asleep, dreaming that Eastern gods dressed in gold were feeding me on nectar and ambrosia that turned me into a fat, happy little Indian baby. What could be more appropriate?

A bell rang at half past three in the morning, and not long after that the prefect switched on both the light and the tape recorder, and handed me a loin-cloth to wear on my way to the shower. Being a guest, I was allowed a hot shower, unlike the others, and while waiting I met the Abbot from Soho once more, and wished him good morning. Outside the guest rooms, devotees lay stretched out on the bare floor in sleeping bags. Clearly theirs was a rigorous regime. Early rising is a feature of Indian ashrams I am told, but there they go to bed early as well.

Downstairs, the dancing, chanting and music were wilder than ever. Up and down they all bounced, although the spiritual master was presumably still in bed. This time I was given a song sheet which included an English translation.

'We are delivering the Western countries, which are filled with impersonalism and voidism.'

'May we not be deprived of the ideal of sitting at the lotus feet of Sri Guru. I will give up criticising other people.'

I felt bound by no such promise, and looked around with sleepy curiosity. Enthusiastic impersonalism seemed to prevail, as always. Who were these young men and women, and how had they come here?

They were proof that happiness is not everything, for their mindless glee must have seemed tragic to their parents. Few of them looked like reformed drug addicts, and I doubt if many of them had been university students. Probably the movement had begun, like so many others, with LSD users seeking a safer form of ecstasy; and had now become established enough to attract ordinary young people. With new names, they obviously felt themselves to be different personalities from Simon or Sandra of the school, shop or office of yesterday.

Excitedly, a group ran past me carrying a nondescript shrub in a flower pot, and with loud chants, a circle formed around it, bowing and worshipping.

'That is Tulasi, our sacred plant,' someone said.

We then stopped dancing and told the beads, chanting ceaselessly, of course. I must have looked all-in, as the prefect came over and whispered that I could go back to bed if I liked.

After a short sleep, I was called downstairs again for 'an important meeting'.

I sat down on the temple floor, and read a pamphlet which told me that in the Manor there could be 'no meat eating, intoxication, illicit sex or gambling'.

A microphone was rigged up in the middle of the floor, and was manned by a severe young man who, shaven head apart, looked exactly like an organising type in a fundamentalist chapel.

Brothers were called up from the audience to him one by one, and congratulated on the record number of points they had earned. Apparently the point system played a large part in Manor life, and the awards were made for salesmanship and fund raising. Worship seemed forgotten for the moment, and a sterner material world emerged, of daily trips to town to sell flowers, records, books and knick knacks, with quotas and honours for top salesmen. Everyone who was congratulated on their points received a round of applause, and the talk was all of fund raising.

'The aim is book distribution,' the stern brother told us, looking as if he ought to have been wearing a grey suit.

During the week, I realised, the devotees were in business for Krishna, and for once were *not* encouraged to use his name. Interrupted sleep probably helped to keep them loyal and unquestioning.

Once the pep talk was over a more relaxed atmosphere crept over the Manor. There was another diatribe against non-Hare Krishnas, who were not only sex-crazed animals, it appeared, but also cocaine addicts for the most part. Then came dancing, sitting on the floor to eat a revolting breakfast, and yet more dancing and chanting.

Standing in the hall, watching the dancers through the glass temple doors as their robes and saris flapped about and their arms waved here and there, I was reminded of bees with loudly buzzing wings. Wherever, I went, the buzz of Krishna-gabble followed me. Devotees sat on the stairs or walked past me, hand busy in bead bag, chanting 'Hare Hare' and 'Rama Rama' in private obsession. In guest room or toilet, the chant was inescapable, following me through chinks in the walls or door. Every corner seemed to have a devotee rattling off his rama ramas, for apparently this was a free period and this was the use they made of their freedom. I felt as if I had shrunk and been admitted to a beehive, but although courteously treated by the bees had no means of understanding their activities. Benign non-human insect faces looked through me as I wandered around, and the buzzing grew and grew.

In the lounge I found a respite, as some of the girls were sitting together talking in real voices, using actual sentences! They spoke almost in whispers, huddled together, and seemed faintly ashamed of not chanting. Well cared for, much-loved children toddled around them and these formed the topic of their conversation. As long as motherhood exists, women can never be as silly as men, as they nearly always put children before theories. Mothers, I have always noticed, form little islands of sanity even in Marxist gatherings.

'I'm so glad we're in the Manor,' one young mother was saying, 'as it's so nice for Gopal. It was awful where we were before, in that crumby room. Yes, [hugging the child] you're in the *guest* room, aren't you?'

However, the ladies left, and the chanters encroached once more. Upstairs I looked out of the window, for it was light by now, and saw how peeling and decrepit the Manor looked, with rubbish dumped in heaps all over the garden. Trying to read my pamphlet, I became aware of a nearby Krishna-drone, and looked up to see a tall young man, his face contorted as if in agony, marching up and down shouting the mantra at the top of his voice. Probably, he was afraid of losing points with Krishna and being relegated to the dog, cat or hog league. Who would not prefer the lowliest animal form to being a Krishna-ite?

'Of all the senses, the tongue is most voracious and uncontrollable,' I read. 'It is very difficult to conquer the tongue in this world.'

But they had done it, the myriad Krishna-bees, who had subjected their tongues to a heavy yoke, that of saying the same words over and over again all their lives for ever. Out I went, to seek fresh air and solitude in the gardens. My shoes were still where I had left them, and as I put them on, I listened to the devotees getting ready to drive off in vans and sell their wares.

One of the stables, I found, was piled up with L.P. records, pictures and other items for selling. I roamed around the grounds, which were not unduly large, but included a field or two, and there were supposed to be cows somewhere. An ornamental stream was choked up with leaves, but at least the grass had been cut. It was a marshy, miserable, rubbish strewn place, or so it seemed that morning. There was a large pond with moorhens that might have looked pretty on a sunny day.

Exploring, I found a round shed that on closer inspection proved to be a shrine for a female deity painted gold. Not far away was a muddy and neglected kitchen garden with empty greenhouses. 'Chant Hare Krishna' was painted in enormous white letters on the brick garden wall. What was this?

Ahead of me, I could see a greenhouse in use, with violet lamps for heating, and plants inside. Someone there must have some sense after all! Pleased, I hurried over to see what was growing.

Wouldn't you know it? There were the wretched sacred plants, Tulasis, all in a row. So much for horticulture. Next I came across a car park, and to my surprise found a real Indian juggernaut cart in it, as used in holy processions. It was painted red and blue, with enormous red wheels of solid wood, a pattern of swans and flowers around it, and a tarpaulin draped over the top. Nearby was a smaller version. Were they pulled by bullocks, or cows or devotees? Did frenzied Krishna-ites from Bolton or Wigan throw themselves under the wheels?

A juggernaut of a different kind stretched from one end of the car park to another, a huge modern container lorry, its engine left running, but with no driver in sight. Steps led up to a door in its side, so I went inside, and found, to my amazement, a self-contained flat, with a kitchen, bunks, and strangest of all, a large temple with a dance floor and a gilded, well decorated altar. The light must have come in through the roof. Clearly the temple and some devotees made journeys all over England, tearing along the motorways with Krishna, and parking wherever the prospects for Krishna consciousness seemed the greatest. Hastily I got out before I was driven away, to become a motorised Krishna-gipsy.

Round the corner, and there were the gates of the Manor driveway and a notice board also decorated with swans. Behind me stood the house, filled with chanting from top to bottom.

Escape, escape! Why should I stay for the whole weekend and risk going mad or being poisoned? I still had the beads in my pocket, so I darted back and hung them on a door handle, and then out I ran into the blessed normality of Letchmore Heath. What expressive faces, full of character, these normal people had!

How marvellous to see a council notice board once again, where even the heading 'Potters Bar Area Planning Sub-Committee' seemed almost rational! Farewell to Krishna, whose devotees seemed to have been haunting my days and nights for years!

I set my hitching thumb into action and walked away through the drizzle down a long country road, my shoes beating out a rhythm as I went, 'Hare Krishna, Hare Krishna, Krishna Krishna, Hare Hare . . .'

[PART SIX]
The Age of Faiths

PREFACE

Not everybody who became a rebel in the nineteen sixties prospered, although many of them did. The BBC, the theatre, the 'Caring Professions', all these filled with rebels, rebelling away to carve niches for themselves and to clasp England in the iron grip of Authoritarian Anarchy. Life was made hard, in the early seventies, for those who didn't want to shock old ladies out of their complacency. Colleges turned conformists from their doors. I regard it as a major triumph of my life that, although of the right age (born in 1941), I never became a hippie. By taking this stance, and by insisting on helping old ladies across the road and standing up for them in buses instead of shocking them, I cut myself off from all that was officially admired in my generation.

Now and again, I would revisit those who had rebelled against Society, and we would compare notes. I found that by being a passive conformist, and letting things happen to me, I could have just as many adventures as those who proudly rebelled. Instead of regarding the drug traffic as a great adventure to take part in, I thought it more admirable and no less daring to try and discourage it. Eventually, many of my old associates began giving up drugs of their own accord. Those who had not been adequately rewarded by Society for their rebellion sought refuge in strange cults.

Emboldened by my experience with the Hare Krishnas, and enriched by my recent success in Fleet Street, I began, in the last days of the Seventies, to explore these cults. Sometimes my explorations took me far from Pupworth, to Edinburgh, that noble and most earnest of cities, and to manor houses haunted by lost souls in the heart of the countryside. When visiting friends I had made at Meadowvale Dell I would often be told of strange goings on at the local Big House. On occasion, old Sussex acquaintances I had known for years would join a cult, and I would go and see them. My journal of these adventures took the name of 'The Age of Faiths'.

Most of the experiences described in this book were written down shortly after they happened, and Part Six is no exception. Re-reading it after five years, I find it has not dated too much. Many worn-out socialist ideals have burst into new life of late, but only for women. Excluded from the vigorous world of the 'feminists' or women who try to be unfeminine, young men seem at a loss for an ideology or a guide to life. Brought up as a patriot, I found it easy to transfer my allegiance from Russia, which I had never seen, to Britain, which I knew very well. Later generations, brought up in the nihilistic atmosphere of rebellion for its own sake, are not so fortunate. Secondary school teachers no longer tend to believe that Russia is Heaven, but assume instead that the whole world is Hell. But I have Hope where the mood seems hopeless, as I believe in a *real* Heaven, and in a spiritual life on earth.

'Mad religions', such as I describe, are still flourishing, and are becoming accepted as normal. Both in Liverpool and in London I have recently seen schoolmistresses, dressed in the robes of guru-devotees, taking young children on outings.

Required reading for the would-be conformist are *Orthodoxy* and *Heretics* by G. K. Chesterton. To descend from the sublime to the ridiculous, Part Six of this volume, as well as describing strange cults, also includes instructions on How To Be a Conformist. As there are very few conformists under seventy years of age in Britain at present, I hope it will be of some help to new recruits. So if you have borne with me so far, I shall sign off with 'The Age of Faiths' and bid you all farewell. I am sitting in my room in a Victorian guest house at the moment, one eye on this manuscript and the other on the electric meter in the corner. When the fire goes out, I shall take my plastic bag, now containing the typewritten autobiography of a gypsy horse-dealer, and wander out into the night in search of change and chips. My readers are welcome to go on to Part Six, bearing in mind that it describes, in the present tense, an age that has almost vanished.

THE AGE OF FAITHS
(From my Diary, 1979)

The Middle Ages may have been the Age of Faith, but the late twentieth century is surely the Age of Faiths. Lunatic religious sects, once the prerogative of California, are now established and increasing their hold all over Britain. In a previous 'Age of Faith', whether medieval or Victorian, these sects would have been seen as an amazing revival of every kind of pre-Christian superstition. As so many members of the sects are unaware of the Christian tradition, perhaps to be post-Christian and pre-Christian is the same experience. Curiously, the new, or revived, superstitions appeal almost exclusively to the young victims of the late Sixties boom in further education. However, these number so many thousands that the 'mad sects' have become a feature of town life.

An odd feature of these sects is that each one seems to glorify its Founder in a Chairman Mao-like manner, with pictures of unpleasant, fat, cynical and totally materialistic Leaders everywhere. The appeal of the sects doesn't seem to be in the doctrine, but in the personalities of the Leaders – personalities which would repel most ordinary people.

When everything is in confusion, when institutions no longer seem to be secure and a country's confidence is shaken, then a madman can become a hero, because of his supreme unshakable self confidence. Luckily the many rival cults, all sneering at each other, prevent a national movement which could create a Hitler in Britain.

Our topsy-turvydom is the result of the destructive fashions of the nineteen sixties. First came the satire craze, which, by means of television, discredited every traditional institution, including the Church. Then came the governmental craze for Pointless Change, which has left most Britons as if shell-shocked, or 'Sixties-shocked', with the feeling that *everything* has been abolished. The satirised institutions are nearly all still there, but people seem to think them unreal now, and to imagine them as either abolished or about to be abolished. Even abstract ideas, such as love and honour, have become unusually vague, and no one seems certain if Good and Evil have been abolished or not.

If ordinary working people feel themselves to be in a vacuum, then how much worse it must be for those uprooted exam-passees of the late Sixties who grew up with these confusions as a background! Most people are kept sane by a feeling of tradition, even if they are not sure if the tradition is discredited or not. But the devotees of the insane cults only have lack-of-a-tradition for a tradition!

Recently a young Welsh policeman told me how amazed he was when he discovered (by way of seances) that the soul and the body could be looked on as two separate parts, and that perhaps the spirit could exist after the body had decayed. Not once did it occur to him as he spoke that his radical new ideas had long been taken for granted in the Christian Church, and had been expounded Sunday after Sunday in every orthodox place of worship in the land.

The Welfare State, with its dreary jargon-ridden language, has obscured the fact that we have an Established Church, and 'the Welfare' has become the rival of Christianity.

Perhaps it is the establishment of the Welfare State that has taken the fire and the faith out of Socialism. Socialism as a substitute for religion has created a mental world of greater intricacy and strangeness than any realms of theology, and this world of the intellect, in its Godless form, has been with us since the eighteenth-century Enlightenment. All of a sudden its impetus seems to have died, and the mental equipment, so to speak, is lying around like useless junk or broken tools. Workmen in Britain now have higher wages than the intellectual socialists, and the novels of Solzhenitsyn have exposed the Workers' Paradise of Russia, which can no longer offer comfort to our anti-patriots.

Instead of turning to the Church of England, and instead of studying realistic politics and old institutions, the radical type of young person now finds fulfilment and conviction in an amazing variety of magical mumbo-jumbo-ish beliefs. I visited a Folk Club recently, and could see how inappropriate the old 'social protest' songs seemed to the young student types who were there. They were the only songs they knew, all part of the revolutionary tradition, yet what was really exciting the patrons was a hand-printed mystical newspaper that was being handed round. One of the articles in it, a rather gushing piece in praise of God, would not have been out of place in a Christian magazine. On the whole, however, a witless playfulness prevailed, and the new slogan that was being repeated aloud was not 'Landlords-Out!' but 'Every Day is Sunday – Everyone is Wally'.

'You can count me out,' I said, leaving quickly.

So socialism as a religion has evidently reached a crisis, if not the end of the road, and I can't say that I'm sorry. It was certainly curious to hear a socialist Prime Minister, in 1975, railing furiously at 'rogue elephant' employers who paid their men *more*.

Young people now talk about God without embarrassment, but are a bit chary of Jesus, preferring 'meditation' to prayer, and reincarnation to a Heavenly reward. A sophisticated person can make his or her mind go blank in meditation, but would feel very silly talking to God. Where students once ranted against 'capitalism', they are now content to complain of 'materialism'. This is not so bad, as they don't seek to exterminate 'materialists'. Probably the Welfare State and the trade unions have caused this change in attitude, as it seems to me that the new student 'enemy' is the rich working man. Some young people seem to turn to rock music and mysticism as if they were the *only* alternatives to a life of Bingo, new cars, package tours and cocktail cabinets. The existence of art, literature, culture and cultured people seems to have escaped them – probably because no on has told them about it.

Materialism can create a keen mood in a country, and so help to stimulate the arts and make a spiritual balance. This is not happening now, as the triumph of socialist thought has either impoverished or wiped out the cultured classes, and the New Money is mostly spent on beer and produces nothing more lasting than a hangover.

'Anti-materialism', on the other hand, is equally dotty. While visiting a friend recently, I stayed talking until late, when a knock came at the door. When it was opened, a young man, frozen with cold, almost fell into the room. He had been living in an empty house, known as 'the squat', and another of the squatters, a madman, had been chasing him round and round with an axe. Totally destitute, he was also on bail on a drugs charge, to add to his troubles, and seemed to be nearly starved. No sooner had he been revived by a cup of tea, and he had thawed out a little, than he began to declaim in ringing tones against materialism!

This is where the leaders of the new religions came in. Anti-materialist young people can be persuaded to sell all their belongings and donate the money to the cult, which in turn offers commune accommodation. The Divine Light Mission and the Children of God both do this, and the lives of their devotees become one long recruitment drive for the cult in question. Now the question arises – how can anybody, however young, be silly enough to believe in the Divine Light Mission or the Children of God?

The key to this silliness is a crucial ingredient in the new mumbo-jumbo, and its name is lysergic acid diethylamide, or LSD. In the late Sixties, the whole evolution of social protest, from 'No Popery' to 'No Property', seemed to have reached its Ideal Form, or end product, in a small pill which you swallow. LSD transformed the soul, apparently, and abolished the Old Adam in us all, to make a Heaven on earth of Noble Savages and Beautiful People, all drugged to the eyeballs and repeating things like 'Peace and Love' with beatific, angelic smiles.

In actual practice, the first dose of LSD seems to induce an unearthly ecstasy, lasting several hours, and which afterwards cannot be described coherently. Later experiments are less and less effective in this way, and lead on to all kinds of delusions, horrors and madness. So eventually the whole culmination of the socialist tradition fizzled out into nothing, as the LSD-takers mostly felt compelled to stop taking the drug.

Always, however, they remembered their first experience of ecstasy, and sought to recreate it by meditation and magic – hence the new religions. Without LSD, the new cults would have halved in their followings, and some may not have come into existence at all. It may be that LSD really does 'increase spiritual awareness' at the cost of *mental* awareness, so that its takers feel very religious but can only appreciate a religion that is ludicrous and insane. However, the desire of most ex-LSD fans seems to be perpetual mindless ecstasy. Obviously their brains are damaged.

(Strangely enough, a member of a Conservative 'Think Tank' once advocated an 'ecstasy pill' as the cheap honours system of the future. As a reward for public service, the unfortunate benefactor would take a pill, no doubt handed to him by the Queen, and at once fall into a mindless ecstasy which would be a form of brain damage in itself. What would Sir Francis Drake have said to that?)

In one way LSD has fulfilled its promise, as so many of its former users are now blissfully happy, and will possibly remain so until their dying day. It seems very sad to me, as so many of them were young people of great promise. Now they are simpletons who can read no books other than those connected with their new religion.

In this post-LSD age, almost the only secular opinions left among the anarchist young, apart from anti-materialism, are wafflings about 'conservation' and 'ecology', which are feeble parodies of age-old Tory sense, and could just as well be described as 'good estate management'. The organised revolutionary societies are still there, but they have lost their vast army of fellow-travellers to the religions.

The concept of God implies Order, as it makes us see ourselves as a part of a properly constructed Creation. Atheists are usually political rebels, but in Britain now we have a whole caste of ex-hippies, who, with clouded minds, are trying to become ordinary people, and to build institutions. They don't realise that Church and State have been *needlessly* discredited, but ignore them as if they were abolished and go searching for a meaning for life among the gurus. Most of the new religions are puritanical about drugs, and give the poor surfeited hippies an excuse to stop taking them without losing face. Even the worst of the new religions must take the credit for weaning young people away from drugs. In fact, many former advocates of drugs who have done great harm to others, turn right round and become terribly self-righteous in criticising their old disciples.

Many former rebels take a mad religion on marriage (or on settling down, rather) as if instinctively trying to make themselves normal. Without the necessary brains, they create only a parody of normality.

Enough of the whys and wherefores – now let us go and take a look at the mad religions.

The average person's idea of a mad religion is the Jehovah Witness. I disagree strongly, as to my mind, the definition of a mad religion, at least in the post-LSD sense, is one in which virtually all the members are young. Sects that were established long before the nineteen sixties in England form no part of my subject, and have no appeal to radical youth. In my opinion, the Jehovah Witnesses are much maligned, and have many saintly people in their ranks. They are far closer to chapel Christianity than most people realise. Religions with church-type meeting halls rather than communes, and with middle-aged and old people well represented, are far too sane, orderly and decent to appeal to the Sixties Lost Generation.

Pentecostal churches, Churches of Christ Scientist (!) and Christadelphian churches are all variants of church and chapel Christianity, their more bizarre features notwithstanding. Spiritualist churches, whose services often consist of displays of magic, whether real or pretended I cannot say, also have respectable all-age congregations. As for out-and-out non-Christians, the Buddhist and Bahai Faith meetings nibble at the edge of the Lost Generation, so to speak, but on the whole are dominated by responsible and genteel older people. Many hundreds of young people are becoming converts to Christian churches, as well as to the new religions, but these are clean-cut conservative types and are not as unique in English history as the followers of the Faiths.

The Faiths I am going to describe are the Divine Light Mission, whose Leader is the young Guru Maharaji; a sect I shall call the Temple of Electrology, which has overtones of a secular 'improve your efficiency' course, and which professes a scientific method; and last of all, the Children of God, who seem at first sight to be everyday Christian evangelists.

I am Church of England in my beliefs, and much of what I saw among the above cults made me laugh. Of course I stifled my laughter at the time, as I was in the most dishonest position of pretending to be a guileless would-be convert to the Faiths. I have been criticised by young atheist ex-students, schoolteachers and the like, for sounding 'superior' as I describe the Faiths. They seemed to respect these Faiths, even without believing in them, in a way that they would never respect, say, the Methodists or the Presbyterians. 'I'm afraid I'm cynical,' a student visitor to an Electrology meeting told me most apologetically – whereas, if ever there was a time for being cynical in, that time was then. I *was* rather surprised by the matter-of-fact way in which working people and farm labourers would direct me to some distant commune, without the trace of a smile or an odd look, so perhaps *all* religions are respected in modern England. There may well be a drawback to Tolerance.

The Divine Light Mission has, as its head, the Guru Maharaji, hailed as 'The Twelve-Year-Old Perfect Master'. As such, he is looked on as the equal of Jesus and Buddha, who were also 'Perfect Masters', and the Guru is vaguely supposed to be their reincarnation. Like them, he is worshipped as God, but his disciples at first disguise this fact by talking to possible converts only about meditation and 'Peace'. The last is a word so overworked of late as to have become meaning-less.

Followers of the young Guru are called 'Premmies', and they live in communes known as 'ashrams'. The cult began in India, flourished in California and reached its height in Britain in the early Seventies. 'Premmies' give up all their worldly goods, which are sold to the public in shops belonging to 'Divine Sales Incorporated'. In addition, the ashram-dwellers go to work and donate all their spare cash to the Movement. The head office in South London is a very busy matter-of-fact place, with office girls rattling away at typewriters – it could easily be mistaken for an employment agency.

Ashrams, I discovered, are very clean, almost over-hygienic places, and the Premmies are well scrubbed and radiant. During the heyday of the cult, the Premmies were almost all ex-university students who had once been outrageous hippies, and were transformed by the Guru to neat, obsessive shop-assistants. However, although in suits, many still had strange drug-crazed eyes, which distinguished them from ordinary people.

Young men in ashrams often talk of their conversion, their renunciation of all worldly goods, and of the day they had their hair cut. It's rather touching, really – the Premmies give up that which is most dear to them, their hair.

Ashrams are free and easy places, and I often used to drop into one in the South of England, where I would get a cup of tea and a chat about the marvellous Guru. Colour photographs of him hung on all the walls, and his day-to-day doings were followed admiringly. Most of the premmies there had been to Sussex University, had taken LSD and then discovered the Guru. I never met one who had not taken the drug, if their own admissions could be trusted. Good-mannered, well-spoken contented young people, they nearly all spoke like this: 'When I was a student, away from home for the first time, life seemed meaningless. I tried everything, every kind of drug, and I was only happy when I found the Guru. Now I'm really happy – it's really wonderful! I have taken knowledge, and now I'm blissed out, and only want to praise the Guru forever! I hear beautiful music all the time inside me . . .'

I would have thought that the university was the place from which to 'take knowledge', but except for the lucky few whose boarding schools have enabled them to withstand life away from home, this seldom seems to be the case.   .

'Taking knowledge' in the Guru-sense, I found, was like this. After meditating and visiting ashrams for a time, the would-be Premmies would seek out a Master from the cult-headquarters. If this person (usually an Easterner) found the convert to be in a state of spiritual readiness, he could impart knowledge in a matter of minutes. This was done by the convert's head being forced back, and the Master's thumbs pressed heavily into his closed eyes. If you try this on yourself, you will find that you see coloured flashes, and no doubt the Masters know all kinds of tricks, for the Premmies say that since taking knowledge in a blaze of wonderful lights, they can hear celestial music inside themselves all day long. I would imagine that this would terminate their usefulness to the world, except as mouthpieces for the Guru Maharaji.

On entering this ashram, I would take off my shoes and leave them at the foot of the stairs, where a regular cobbler's shop-pile usually lay. The house belonged originally to an old lady, but she had apparently become a convert and given it to the Guru. She lived, I was told, in the basement, but I never saw her. Everyone I saw there was young. The 'house-mother', an ex-student who worked very hard as full-time housekeeper, would make me a cup of tea, and when the others came back from work or from evangelising, we would 'go into satsang', or worship.

'Satsang' was held always in a special room of the spotless house, with cushions on the floor for kneeling or sitting cross-legged on, and a whiff of incense in the air. Guru pictures looked down complacently. Some were not of the Guru himself, but of his relatives.

Generally there was a lot of chanting, and a toothy young man would strum a guitar and sing a Guru folk song, 'We love you, Guru'. Everyone would join in except me, but by politely doing nothing as amiably as I could, I suppose I gave tacit approval to the 'satsang'.

As in all ashrams, there was a shrine at one end of the room, on the floor amid cushions. A framed photograph of the Guru was propped up on a miniature platform, and everyone faced this as they sang and chanted. But *this* ashram had something special – the Guru's sock! There it lay reverently on a cushion, and gifts, or sacrifices, were placed before it. It was a very clean white ankle-sock, such as schoolgirls wear, and its offerings on one occasion were a stick of pink rock and a couple of cooking apples. These had been given to the Premmies on their door-to-door begging excursions, and they ate them afterwards.

First of all, they abased themselves towards the sock, however. On their knees, their hands on the ground before them, their foreheads almost touching the floor in traditional salaaming style, they prayed and worshipped away most fervently. Some groaned aloud with rapture, others cried 'Oh Guru!' in emotion-laden voices. To myself, I composed a hymn for them to sing:

'Hail to thee, O mystic sock!
Please accept this stick of rock.'

However, I didn't tell them this. To be fair, it was not the sock they were worshipping, but its former owner, and perhaps through him in some zig-zag way, God.

One day I said to the Premmies, 'All you people have such a strange, distinctive look in your eyes.'

'Yes,' agreed the toothy young man, pleased. 'And now you're getting it too! You'll soon be one of us.' After that, I did not return for some time.

When I did so, I found the ashram to be sadly reduced in numbers. Instead of being all-English, many of the members were Persians, who were not very friendly and seemed inscrutable to me. I was not able to find what devious paths had brought them there.

What had happened, I learned, was this. The incredibly rich Perfect Master, no longer a small child, had up and married his beautiful blonde secretary! Pictures of the couple were everywhere, along with their baby. The Guru's wife, Durga, seemed a soulful-looking girl, and this change of ashram-picture gave the house a faint echo of Catholicism and nativity pictures. For some reason, the English Premmie I spoke to seemed to connect the marriage with the ashram's decline, although he seemed greatly to venerate Durga and the child.

From other sources I learned that the Guru's mother had been shocked at the mixed marriage, and had not only ceased to help her son's Mission, but had denounced it and left, creating a Schism. She now claimed *herself* to be the Perfect Master – or Perfect Mistress, perhaps – but had few followers outside the East.

A very flourishing ashram, I found, was the one in Edinburgh. Edinburgh is a most dramatic city, and its earnest, high-minded character, light years away from that of Glasgow, makes it a centre for religion in general, the cults included. The Edinburgh Premmies could sing traditional songs in folk-style, as well as Guru songs, and often gave free entertainments at the city hospitals. One of the girls, who had a landed gentry background, could draw beautifully, and she and her friends would go on 'soup runs' with an Anglican Mission, looking after down-and-outs. Their worship and way of life were similar to those of the English Premmies. They had the usual altar-with-photograph, some worked at the Divine Sales shop, and almost everyone seemed to have taken LSD.

Everyone living in the ashram was young, and they seemed to be organised by a rather officious young student, who was fond of paperwork and could easily have been taken for a Young Conservative. I rather doubt if he had taken drugs, and he helped to run a busy office in the ashram. At the meetings, some older people turned up, and a 'regular' was a very grand old lady who was treated as a Queen, although she never spoke and was blind and crippled. Perhaps she had helped the Movement in some way. Two haggard middle-aged ladies had apparently popped in in the hope that 'meditation' would cure their deep unhappiness. One had a brutal husband, and the other, who looked bohemian, said that she had never got over her 'last relationship'. Probably the absurdity of Guru-proceedings, of which meditation forms only a part, would soon drive them out to face their problems as best they could.

Three Premmie-children, all very good looking, lived in the ashram. One of them, a little blond boy called Ben, had come all the way from America. His mother was a rather bleached, strained-looking Californian folk-singer type girl, whose marriage had gone wrong. She had become a Premmie in America, and had come to Britain armed with a list of towns with ashrams. The Edinburgh branch had a vacancy and so the young lady, laden with luggage and clutching Ben by the hand, had arrived by train during a violent rainstorm.

Not knowing where to go, she had struggled with Ben and belongings up and down the many ancient steep stone stairways that descend from the Royal Mile down the rock to the fruit market below. It was pouring with rain, the steepness of the steps cannot be imagined by those who haven't climbed them, and all the time she was pathetically asking passers-by the way to 'the ashram', and being directed here and there by the bewildered burghers.

Let her take up the tale now:

'And so, in all that rain, I just sat down on one of my trunks and cried out, "Oh, Ben, Ben, where is our home?"'

'And what do you think? Straight away he answered, "Home is inside you, Mummy."'

'It was so true, I just gasped! It was the Guru – the Guru talking through Ben! Isn't that incredible? After that, I knew I had been wrong to worry, and sure enough, in the end, we found the ashram.'

Probably Ben had learned the patter from his life of being carted from ashram to ashram. During 'satsang', when everyone was talking and singing about Peace and Love, Ben played loud and violent war games with toy soldiers and guns. Everyone smiled at him affectionately, and he was the pet of the place.

One day, when I was there, a wild man knocked at the door. He was a young down-and-out who had been given the address by one of the soup-runners, who had found him in a derelict house. He was a tall, strong young man in a huge black coat, and when he was asked to take off his shoes, was embarrassed by the state of his socks and feet. Sitting among us, cross legged on a cushion, he at once began his story, in a Scottish accent which I cannot imitate. As he spoke, he gazed at everyone wild eyed, with the desperation and nervous violence of a mad killer. It was a gaunt raw face, very Scottish in its combination of black hair and staring blue eyes, and it would not have been out of place in an unusually macabre old Dickens illustration.

Without preamble, the young man remarked that he had just come out of prison. He had, he said, been sentenced to three years in Parkhurst for peddling LSD. His girlfriend had persuaded him to do this, and he had taken all the blame when he was caught. That was his story, but I daresay there was more to it than that. After serving his time, he had returned to *his* home town, Edinburgh, but his family were gone.

Mentally scarred by prison and LSD, he had taken to walking up and down the streets all night long, pacing restlessly for no reason, and sleeping among tramps when exhausted. The police kept pulling him in for questioning, as there had been a spate of burglaries, but they always turned him loose again. This sounded convincing, as I've noticed the police tend to fight shy of the insane, and who can blame them?

'Walking, walking. Ah just keep walking,' said the tormented one, with a silly laugh. 'Ah wish Ah knew whit had happened to mah old girlfriend. Anyway, I'd like to see if meditation can do me some good.'

The Premmie girls soothed him, sat him by the fire and made him tea, and he was quite overwhelmed, breaking into a goofy grin. There was such a contrast, he said, betweeen their kindness and the grimness of prison, where he had always been in trouble for not obeying those rules that didn't seem to make sense to him. This attitude ensured that he served his time the hard way, and the ashram was like a new world, a Heaven, for him.

Soon he was as mellow as any of them, meditating away and looking forward to 'taking knowledge', getting 'blissed out', and hearing internal music.

'Do you think you could let him stay the night here?' I asked the artistic girl.

'No', she replied in a matter-of-fact voice, and went on talking about the Guru.

The Californian girl was getting very friendly with the stranger, but she later told me that he was 'still tripping' – that is, taking LSD while he was meditating there. She spoke in a voice of horror, so I asked if she thought LSD was bad for people.

'Very bad indeed, to keep on taking it,' she replied. 'Of course, like everyone else, I used to take it myself, but we all stopped years ago.'

Meanwhile, the drugged stranger was telling about how he had sought the Governor's permission to grow a moustache, had grown it and then shaved it off again. Furious, the Governor had summoned him to the office and demanded to know why he had abused his privilege by shaving off his hard-won moustache. The newcomer seemed set to ramble on about prison half the night, as a preamble to his literal ramblings of the streets in the freezing autumn small hours. I made my goodbyes, and went downstairs to put on my shoes, the one good pair (I prided myself) among all the battered Premmie sandals.

The shoes were cut to ribbons, probably by the mad stranger! That served me right for snooping into innocent ashrams and prying out the secrets of the Premmies!

Elmer Fuddard, an American, is the founder and leader of what I shall call the Temple of Electrology. Electrology is obliged to call itself a religion to prevent itself from being closed down in Britain, as there is evidence that its followers become insane. From what I have seen, however, I think it more likely to appeal to people who are *already* slightly mad. At first Electrology tried to pose as a 'science' for atheists and as a 'religion' for mystics, and it still savours strongly of an American efficiency course. If its own literature is to be believed, it has a following among dynamic executives in the States. In England its followers sometimes appear to be streamlined whizz-kids of efficiency, but always in pursuit of ridiculous ends.

Most of Elmer Fuddard's disciples are fond of space stories. Some of them claim that these stories are *true*, and are either unconscious accounts of the author's adventures in a previous incarnation, or else have somehow *become* true by having been thought of. Electrologists believe that a mental picture springs into physical existence on some other plane. An encyclopaedia could be made of what Electrologists believe. In fact, many *have* been made, and the poor Electrologists have to pay for them! A complete Electrology course would cost over two thousand pounds, easily, and take years to complete. Books, all by Elmer Fuddard and his staff, are required reading, and must be bought, not borrowed.

If anyone could last out the whole course, they would in theory become a Human God with unlimited powers. The idea that 'God is *you*' seems to have great appeal to helpless, futile individuals. There is a massive chart of all the Levels to be attained, and it makes a most daunting sight, written as it is in Electrological jargon that has to be learned. Few, if any, of the Electrology workers have completed the course, and many who recruit others have barely been recruited themselves.

First of all, the convert has to do the FAE Course. These initials stand for 'Fuddard Apprentice Electrologist', for although recruits are told that they are going in for self-improvement, the courses are all geared to make them part of the Fuddard Organisation. So no matter how mad they end up, there will be a place for them in this ever-expanding empire.

Electrologists like to surround themselves with photographs of the mighty Elmer. There he sits in his classic pose, a bald fleshy-faced man of fifty-odd, with his arms folded and a narrow-eyed, contemptuous sneering leer on his face. He is very fond of hunting and shooting, and conducts most of his business from his tent in the Rockies. His personal assistants wear a curious game warden's uniform, which sets them apart as the Electrological élite. They are known as the Trackers. In the Electrology magazine, 'Shh, Be Very Quiet', there has appeared a series of articles on the 'Mighty Hunter from the East', which, it is hinted, is Fuddard himself. The magazine is a curious mish-mash of technological-sounding jargon and bits of Buddhism, the latter looking very out of context in Elmer F's world of tape recorders and patented electric devices.

Bits and pieces of Elmer's vast mental structure have been borrowed from Freud and Darwin. Psycho-analysts believe that incidents in early childhood affect a person in later years, and Darwinians believe that man evolved from jelly-like creatures up through fishes, reptiles and lower mammals. Electrologists go one better than both, and believe that we are all affected, mostly for the worst, by incidents that happened in previous *incarnations*, and that incarnations follow the evolutionary scale, so that each person's *soul* once resided in a jelly fish, sea urchin, spiny anteater and so on. No wonder we're a funny lot, if we're saddled with complexes belonging to a whole zoo! What kind of problems worry a sea-urchin? Never mind, according to Elmer F., 'scientific auditting' can wipe out the whole menagerie of complexes, and make us into super-beings, or Mighty Warriors. (MWS for short.)

Auditting is a skilled job in the Electrological set-up. The auditor is the instructor who guides each recruit, by means of gruelling inter-views, higher and higher up the 'MW Levels.' The FAE course only takes three weeks to complete, and the student who goes on, finds himself obliged to use an Elmer-meter. This is a machine patented by Elmer Fuddard and is only made by Electrologists, who don't sell them to unbelievers. It is a small lie detector-like device, and the auditted one has to hold a wire in each hand and allow a small charge of electricity to run through him, while shocking or surprising questions are asked him. A needle flickers up and down a dial on the middle of the Elmer-meter, and this shows how much spiritual progress the trainee has made. If the trainee sticks this out, he becomes an auditor himself one day and can do it to others.

I have seen the programme of the FAE course, which can be taken at any of the Electrology branches all over Britain. More advanced courses have to be taken at the British headquarters, Greychamber Grange in Wiltshire. 'Communication' is the main theme of the course, and the Fuddard Apprentice and the 'coach' or auditor, have to stare each other in the eyes for long periods, without blinking or talking. The apprentice has to rid himself of 'the desire to seem interesting' in conversation. Then the 'coach' has to fire silly questions at him, requiring 'Yes' and 'No' answers only, rather like a game of 'Simon Says'. When the victim – I mean apprentice – says the wrong answer, the coach shouts 'Flunk!' at him. Elmer Fuddard, although I'm told that he fancies himself as an English squire when he's at Greychamber Grange, peppers all his writings with slangy, patronising Americanisms. In the final stages of the course, the coach interposes 'startling comments' from a special list into the conversation, to see how the student handles them. I'd love to know what these comments are, but my education in Electrology didn't take me as far as this!

Now a short digression is in order, about an unusual hobby of the student-hippie generation, who are now mostly in their forties. This hobby is 'astral-travelling'. Under the influence of LSD or of strong mental concentration, the astral traveller can fly out of his body as a ghost and have all kinds of adventures, and then return to his physical self once more. This idea, understandably, had great appeal to very many young people. Some say the soul is connected to the body by an invisible thread that breaks when the body dies. Electrologists must think this thread is elastic, for they tell incredible tales of souls journeying through space and safely returning to their unconscious bodies days later.

Astral travellers very often seem to have begun their wanderings under the influence of LSD. The sensation of being a floating soul is one of the effects of the drug. Whether astral travelling is a delusion, hallucination or real, it is obviously very dangerous to a person's sanity – if, that is, it is possible for a sane person to go in for it at all. For a time, in the late Sixties, it seemed to be the twentieth-century counterpart of Victorian dreams of adventure, exploring *real* mountains and jungles.

In a most respectable university, a few years ago, a lecturer pleaded for one of her pupils who had failed his exams, saying, 'It's not his fault, he was out of his body at the time! He has been doing some wonderful experiments in astral travelling.'

A thoroughly LSD-soaked young girl I know claims to be expert at this new form of locomotion. She told me, 'Once I left my body and saw my friend Roger asleep on the divan. I decided to go into him, to see what it was like. As soon as I did, he leaped up and gave a terrible shriek, so that I flew out again. He rushed out of the house and ran down the road screaming, and I never saw him again. You know, I don't think there was room in him for both of us.'

Astral travelling is a favourite talking point of Electrologists. It is to perfect the art they learned under LSD that many people go in for Electrology. However, in Elmer Fuddard's writings, there is very little on the subject. Perhaps he doesn't want to commit himself too much. In the correspondence columns of 'Shh, Be Very Quiet', nearly all the letters are about wonderful experiences while astral travelling, written in a gushing and naive style. Electrologists, according to their letters, can appear as ghosts by operating tables and guide the surgeon's hand to save their loved ones. They can fly all over the place, and alter the weather by will jpower. Another trick is, in ghost form, whispering messages and opinions to people they want to influence. They can also recognise malignant ghosts of other people, and talk to them or banish them. As well, in more solid form, they can successfully 'audit' their dogs, cats and goldfish, and converse with them in American English. Most of these letter writers are American, and they can also make lost objects reappear miraculously. (So can I, by finding them.) Despite the horrors of Elmer F's jargon, his followers certainly live in a rich mental world. Too rich and too 'mental' for me, I'm afraid!

My first introduction to Electrology was not to the official Greychamber Grange variety, but to a cheap backstreet Electrologist in Sussex, near Pupworth. He had learned his craft from Elmer F's organisation, and had then gone freelance, catering for those who had neither the time nor the money for 'established' Electrology. An elderly married man, he ran a 'Do it yourself' shop by day, and gave Electrology lessons and individual private auditting in the evenings. His father had been a music hall entertainer, and he had some annoying Cockney-isms, but he was not too bad a fellow, and very sincere.

His 'regulars' were a former university student well pickled in LSD and now a builder's labourer; a seedy middle-aged layabout; a very well-dressed artistic man in his late thirties, who drew nothing but comic fish in human poses (very good they were, too) and two former grammar school girls, with children but no husbands or steady boyfriends. These girls had ended up in third-rate council blocks and lived off Social Security. They had been introduced to LSD by the student a long time before, and were now trying to give up drugs and to find an alternative ecstasy in Electrology.

I think LSD had affected one of their children, as this little girl seemed very odd and uncanny. On one occasion when I was there, she clearly said 'I keep on losing my body,' in an irritated voice.

Losing the sight and feeling of one's body is a typical experience of sufferers from both LSD and rabies. The girl's mother was also a bit strange and sat listening to Electrology tapes while sucking her thumb avidly.

Rows and rows of tiny terraced houses, two up and two down, with basement kitchens facing the backyards, sloped up one side of the hill, all painted in bright colours, like South Wales without the grimness. This picturesque neighbourhood was Electrology Country. My destination was a house in the middle of a long narrow street with corner shops and a pub at each end. Old insurance-plaques, from the days of private fire brigades, adorned most of the house fronts.

I was welcomed to the gathering, and we sat round a table and listened to tapes of Elmer Fuddard talking nonsense. For although my host had broken with the Greychamber Grange officials, he was a great believer in the 'pure doctrine', straight from the mouth of Elmer with no bureaucratic middlemen.

Every time someone couldn't understand a word, he would stop the machine and explain it. 'Never go past a word you can't understand' is one of the maxims of Electrology. When he started out learning from Elmer's tapes, the do-it-yourself man had been puzzled by the word 'figure'.

'Figure, figure, figure!' Elmer commanded on one of the tapes, meaning 'think'.

Not understanding this Americanism, the poor man had tried imagining figures of eight and other numbers, but had eventually got the hang of it. On my visit, he gave a talk on Sympathy. One of his own maxims was 'Sympathy must be ruled out of the case'.

This seemed to go with the Darwinian strain, as how can there be a Survival of the Fittest, and hence evolution, if people and animals persist in being kind to one another? Electrologists believe that by using Elmer's techniques, Man can evolve from 'Homo Sapiens' to 'Homo Newdawnicus'.

'If you see someone drowning, it's plain daft to jump in to save them if you might drown yourself!' we were told. 'It's *you* that matters, not other people! *You* are important, not some fool who can't even keep himself from drowning. Jesus was clever enough in some ways, but not in saying you must lay down your life for others.' There was more in the same vein, all about the Sin of Sympathy. We were told not to address sympathetic remarks to the bereaved or sick. I mentioned that that was a first-class recipe for being hated.

'If they hate you, more fool them – it's *you* that's important,' I was told.

Part of me agreed that I *was* important – begone Satan!

Later the Elmer-meter was produced, and when I declined to use it, my host benignly explained that it was due to some accident back in my seaslug days. After some chit-chat, during which he referred to his exteriorising powers, he let the thumb-sucking girl use the machine. This she did with her usual dreamy smile.

'You want to kill your baby!' the do-it-yourself man suddenly shouted at her.

She smiled goofily, and the needle swung up and down, proving something. The statement was not meant to be true, but to shock and evoke a response.

At that moment, Mrs Electrologist came in with tea and cakes on a tray. Her husband relaxed, and showed me a book he had written. It was his autobiography, and as Electrology had given him perfect recall, it began in the womb. I read it later, and it was a remarkable document that could well be published, about growing up in the nineteen twenties in poor neighbourhoods. Nothing in the naïve style suggested a spiritual person; rather a bawdy cynicism prevailed, a bit over-done, especially as it was all in Cockney. Electrology was not mentioned in it.

I left on the best of terms with everyone, and I later heard that the former university student had taken to Official Electrology and had gone completely insane. LSD was the root of his trouble, as he had the misfortune of being a 'progressive rock' fan in the late Sixties.

Edinburgh, that city on a rock, was the scene of my next Electrological encounter, a year later. Just off the Royal Mile, handy for the shops and university, was a doorway with a big placard outside: 'Free Personality Test'. Above the doorway was an insignificant sign reading 'Church of Electrology'. This was the official branch.

Going up the narrow stairs I found the rooms above absolutely crowded out with shop and office girls wasting their lunch break by doing the Personality Test. Such tests are irrestible to young girls, as a glimpse into their magazines will testify. To know one's own personality! Just what every girl starting work in the exciting city would like to know! No, what *every* girl would like! What wonders and riddles would be revealed!

None of these girls knew of the connection with Electrology. The staff, also youngsters, were very harassed by the queues. All the rooms were full, and people were sitting on chairs in the corridor. Many of the girls were complaining that they had to go back to work, and that they hadn't expected it to take so long. They were told to come back in the evening, and some of them said that they had had their test days ago, and still were being told to come back again and again. Finally I was ushered into a room with a big table, and took my place at it to fill in the Personality Test. Most of the other busy scribblers were vivacious working girls, and a few young men looked like failed students.

As for the test, it was the usual magaziney sort, only much longer. You had to tick one of three squares for 'Yes', 'No' and 'Maybe', and the questions were about feeling odd-man-out at parties and so on, with a touch of 'Are people influenced by you?' Similar inane questions are given to Tech. students, as often as not, to see if they are suitable for their chosen careers. Quiz-makers should realise that there are plenty of excellent people who *don't like* parties, let alone want to make an impression at them. I tried to answer the quiz honestly, but there were so many questions that I kept losing count, as there were two sheets of paper, one for answers only. When I had finished the space for answers, there were ten questions left over, but I handed it in all the same. Apparently each paper took a long time to mark, and I was told to come back the next day. However I had already gathered that *everybody's* personality was found to be 'wrong', and that they were promised new and better ones if they paid five pounds for the FAE Course. This course would recruit them into the Fuddard Organisation, and those who persevered would become fully paid Personality Testers themselves.

When I returned, I was told to sit in the same room as the next wave of quiz-fillers-in, and wait for my name to be called out. To while away the time, I went into a 'Scarlet Pimpernel' act, and wrote out several messages which I handed out to the entrants, with my finger to my lips to prevent discovery. The robust Scottish shop-girls roared with surprised laughter to find out that they were in the clutches of Electrologists, who would find their personalities wanting, charge them five pounds and then attempt to plug them into Elmer-meters. I wrote out several more messages and slipped them among the quiz papers for late-comers. Luckily, the neat, flustered young Fuddard-ites were all in a back room, marking the Tests.

Everyone began to scoff at the Tests after that, and I felt that my time on earth had not been wholly in vain. A girl who hoped to get into Sussex University (poor thing) told me that a friend of hers had gone mad after taking up Electrology. An unkempt young man, who looked as if he would spend his life hoping to get into some university or other, asked me about Elmer Fuddard and his beliefs. I replied in as horrifying a vein as I could manage, all about Elmer-meters, exteriorising and reincarnation, but to my annoyance his eyes shone and he said, 'Great!'

I took a deep breath and had just about managed to disprove

reincarnation to my own satisfaction, when someone called my name. Bidding farewell to my new friends, I went into a small office room to learn the result of my Test.

A very fierce young man confronted me, sitting at a desk. He wore a brown suit and spectacles, and he asked me to sit down. My personality was displayed before me in the form of zig zags on a graph paper. Heavens knows what it said, as I had got all the numbers of my answers muddled up.

My Grand Inquisitor glared.

'You have answered your Test very honestly,' he said. 'There is the result – a dreadful, deplorable Personality. Look, I'll show you.'

And indeed each zig-zag pointed to some dreadful trait of character. Different aspects of Personality were printed along the edge of the paper and I excelled in all the worst of them.

'Are you satisfied, knowing how rotten your Personality is?' the youth demanded.

'Well, look, I've not done too badly as to "Sense of Humour!" '

'That's not "Sense of Humour", that's "Manic Glee"!' he rapped out, scowling.

'I still don't think I'm too bad,' I boasted.

'Let me see. At a party, do you join in the fun, or stand to one side, alone?'

'Well, I don't like parties or dancing. I prefer a good book.'

'In other words, you don't join in the fun! Oh, you can be cocky, you can act brash, but at the bottom, you know you can't Communicate.'

Taking my cue, I acted cocky and brash at first, and then broke down and asked for help in improving my Personality.

'How do you do it? You know everything about me,' I told him in mock-meekness.

I regretted my play-acting as I said this, for he swelled in such unholy pride at his supposed power, and his glasses flashed out such an expression of triumph, that I saw I had spoilt his Personality. Over-confidence, however, might cause his villainy to be more transparent to late-comers. Smugly, he told me to go next door to sign up for the Electrology course that was my only hope.

An efficient-looking office girl took my name, and I told her that my Test had proved negative.

'We can give you a new Personality,' she said brightly. 'We can start right now, if you like.'

She lost interest when I said I had no money on me, and would rather do the course at some other branch, as I had to leave Edinburgh. When I was safely outside I went for a long walk to unscramble my brain, and resolved to leave Electrology alone for a while, although my curiosity about Elmer Fuddard's cult was by no means satisfied.

One fine day, a few months later, I presented myself at Greychamber Grange, feeling rather like Bertie Wooster arriving at a country house full of Aunts. But I had no Jeeves to help me. The Grange was a lopsided neo-Gothic edifice with a great many pointy-roofed towers. I was told that an Albanian Count had once lived there. A new annexe was built like a small castle, shining white and a startling proof that modern architects can make fine buildings, even if rich eccentrics to commission them are few and far between.

Inside, the castle became an undistinguished complex of classrooms and offices, and here I went to announce myself to Reception, where a very normal-looking young lady sat at a typewriter.

She despatched me to another desk and another girl, this time an American, who eagerly told me of a new all-in course I could take for forty pounds. When I revealed I couldn't afford it, she suddenly mentioned the FAE course, which I agreed to take. Everyone doing advanced Electrology courses has to go to Greychamber Grange and to take lodgings at the nearby town at their own expense, as well. The Grange recommends certain boarding houses and commune-flats in town. No sooner had I been welcomed to Greychamber Grange than I was sent to a wooden hut annexe to buy the expensive books that are required reading.

The bookseller seemed to be a horribly mercenary man, but I fobbed him off with a promise to pay the next day. Most of the other Electrologists going busily about their errands looked like young secretaries and girl pop fans, quite innocent looking. Quite a few male Indian and Negro students were there, and the few Western young men were ex-hippie-looking, with some smart, rich-looking Scandinavians. Coloured immigrants, with their various religious backgrounds, must arrive at mad religions by very tortuous mental routes.

Children of Electrologists were doing odd-jobs about the place. It is part of the Electrology belief that children must be treated as grown-ups and made to do everything themselves. Meanwhile the grown-ups play silly games like children. For children with the misfortune of having Electrology parents, it's probably as well that there is no Electrology Sunday School or religious training for children, as even the hardest housework and drudgery must be better by comparison. The children I saw, aged five to about eleven, all looked most responsible. I have been in Electrology households where small children were treated over-strictly and very roughly, with no consideration made for their fears of the dark and of getting lost or hurting themselves.

Less useful than the children at Greychamber Grange were the Trackers, who had worked at Elmer Fuddard's hunting camp, and swanked about the place in uniform, humiliating those of humbler rank.

While waiting for my Ethical Clearance Test, I browsed around the library, noticing that many of the tributes to Elmer by grateful converts were from South Africans with Dutch names. Electrology must have something that appeals to Boers. At last a very dark smartly-dressed Negro told me that my interviewer was ready.

I was asked three questions by a middle-aged lady who seemed to be in a hurry. Did my parents object to my studying Electrology? Had I ever taken harmful drugs? Had I ever been under psychiatric treatment?

My answer to all three questions was 'No', and in a few minutes I was Ethically Cleared.

An assistant showed me through a door, I descended some steps into a large classroom and met my new teacher, Angela. She was a brisk, pleasant-faced red-haired lady, a few years older than myself, and reminded me instantly of the better sort of Infant School Teacher. Under her care, I and the rest of my class reverted at once to being Infants.

'Class!' she announced, clapping her hands for silence. 'We have a new student today!'

I stood up, and everyone applauded me politely. Then I sat down again, when Angela had told them my first name. Everyone was on first-name terms, but I had a strong inclination to call Angela 'Miss'.

'Now class,' my teacher continued, 'I have noticed that many of you are just wandering outside when your work is finished. This is bad for discipline, it causes confusion, and in future you must ask if you wish to leave the room.'

Angela then told me to go next door and collect my tapes, which had to be signed for, played and returned and signed for again. Tape recorders were everywhere, and this is how the lessons were learned. Many different classes were squashed into the same room, with innumerable teachers, and pupils wearing head-phones. Desks were arranged in rows, with pupils facing their auditors and holding Elmer-meters. Few of the auditors, teachers and instructors would have looked unusual in a crowd. Most were quite ordinary-looking English middle-aged women, some wearing black gowns that added an extra mark of distinction. I could easily have believed that they were Oxford dons.

One unusual pupil was a toy rabbit, which was strapped into an Elmer-meter and was undergoing a serious interrogation. The interrogator, a young man, was probably practising to be an auditor. Others, who were ahead of me in the FAE course, were reading excerpts from *Alice in Wonderland* with great solemnity.

Alice in Wonderland about summed it up. Nothing I saw in the classroom was sinister. The Elmer-meters are not painful instruments, apparently. Rather, just as in Lewis Carroll's book, everyone was very busy doing nonsense, with enormous formality. It seemed such a waste of time and intellect. My classroom was a Hall of Nonsense.

At the end of the school day, one of the few older pupils, a silver-haired woman with a tragic and sensitive face, stood up and gave a speech of fervent thanks.

'It's so marvellous to be able to find the time to read all these books,' she said.

Of course all the books in the place were Electrology publications, with the sole exception of *Alice*. She could have saved money and read the *Alice* books at her own fireside, as the reverend author intended.

The tapes I had listened to were an introduction to Electrology. Once introduced, I lost all desire for a lengthy friendship, and my first lesson was my last. Curiosity killed the cat, after all.

Poor Angela! My faithful teacher travelled all the way to the false address I had given, in a far-off town, to pop a scribbled note through the door asking why I had not returned. False addresses are necessary to mad religion investigators, to keep the endless pamphlets at bay. Nevertheless, I feel guilty to this day.

Near the castle, in the Grange grounds, stands the shop where cups of tea and small cakes are sold. This is a shed-like building among the rhododendrons, very dingy, and with no seats. It has become a centre for the scruffier Electrologists – the obvious ex-hippies, unmarried mothers with their children, and hangers-on who are not taking any course at all, and might still be taking drugs. Edinburgh accents often predominate, but the general atmosphere is more that of the easy-going back-street Electrologist than of Greychamber Grange efficiency.

Among the food and odds and ends offered for sale I noticed great stacks of white jars marked 'Vitamins' and looking very home-made. Perhaps the trainees are required to buy them. Therein lie mysteries.

While I stood drinking my tea, I was approached by two Grange students who were doing a survey on Electrology. After answering their questions I was approached by two other equally serious students who were doing a survey on the survey! Drinking up quickly, I fled before being interviewed for the survey on the survey on the survey. So much for Electrology.

Visitors to London's theatreland are sometimes approached by rough young delinquent-looking youths who push leaflets at them. These youngsters are working for the Children of God, and some of them are full-time members of that sect. Girl members are less alarming, but no less peculiar, and turn up at most summer-tourist centres, such as Victoria station, armed with the cartoon-strip leaflets called 'Mo Letters'.

Children of God sell all their possessions and donate the money to the cult, as is customary among mad religionists. One dark-haired girl in Portobello Market told me that it didn't matter, as God gave them everything they wanted.

She meant this literally, and went on to say, 'I gave away all I had, and then just prayed for a fur coat, and one appeared on my bed all by itself.'

Many of the Children of God-girls cultivate 'come to bed eyes', and seem to be trying to seduce possible converts! However, the eyes really mean 'come to the Children of God', and this is a technique laid down in the manual by Moses David, the Founder. He is the Mo who wrote the eccentric 'Letters'. Some Children play guitars and sing in folk-style, to attract the customers. Their favourite Mo-hymn is called 'You Have to Be a Baby'.

Far from London, in a seaside town near Pupworth, I was minding my own business when two young mothers with push-chairs stopped me and enquired after my soul, offering me a leaflet about Jesus. I thought that they were Billy Graham-style evangelists at first.

'I can't get saved now,' I told them politely, ''cos I'm going to the pub on the corner to have a cottage pie and a glass of lager and lime for my lunch. You wouldn't like me to pray and then go in a pub, would you?'

'We don't mind!' one of the girls said. 'Our Lord used to drink wine. If you don't want to pray now, never mind – read the Bible when you get home. Make sure it's the King James' version you read.'

I was thunderstruck. This was surely Anglicanism! Could the attitudes of my own adopted religion, once the Faith of wine-loving scholars, have inspired a youthful evangelical movement? Over my cottage pie and frothy green-cool bubbling lager I examined their leaflets and found that they were Children of God, and very dotty indeed. Another illusion shattered!

A few weeks later, I met one of the girls again, this time without her baby. She was holding hands in a circle with two very uncouth young men with hunched ape-like shoulders and a shabby, mad appearance, and all three were chanting 'Thank you, Jesus!'

They were in the middle of the pavement on a crowded street, but no one took any notice of them. When they had finished, I stepped forward and introduced myself. They explained that they had been asking Jesus which part of town to evangelise in, and at once asked me for money, saying that they lived from day to day on contributions. I paid them in kind by taking them into a chip-shop, where we sat down and I encouraged them to talk about themselves.

'My name's Deuteronomy, and this is my friend Psalms from Southampton,' one of the young men told me. They had taken new names on becoming Children of God. The young lady was called Ruth Valiant, and she refused to tell me her previous name, shuddering at the thought of her life before salvation. She had been a hippie, wandering around North Africa with a drug-happy boyfriend and their baby, who was now called Praise Hannah. Something had happened, and the boy had deserted her in Spain, where she met the Children of God and joined them. As her accent took on a strong American tinge whenever she spoke of religion, I think she must have been converted by someone from that country, probably while she was in a daze of despair. There was no baptism – the Children are saved in the Spirit. Ruth's mother kept in touch with her – the anguish of parents whose children turn mad-religionist is often overlooked in these days of 'tolerance'.

Psalms and Deuteronomy could give me no coherent account of themselves, but they *did* give me a lot of literature. Like all 'Mo Letters', these gave no address, but a Box Number and a 'phone number. Psalms, Deuteronomy and Ruth hurried away to catch up on their evangelising, which was their mission in life, and I rang up the number on the leaflet, found out the address, and made an appointment to call.

When I arrived, I found the house to be part of a vast council estate at the back of town. This surprised me, as most commune-houses are donated by once-wealthy converts to the Faiths. By what process can a religion obtain a council house? The man in charge was a young American with an English wife, but he didn't seem to have been there long. As usual with such religious houses, it was very clean, tidy and orthodox inside, with not much decoration – perhaps a reaction from hippie squalor and daubed wall-paintings.

Inside I met Ruth Valiant and another two girls, some small children and a young man from Germany who played a guitar. Apparently I was in a 'Nursery Colony', for Children of God with children of their own. Commune-houses were called 'colonies', I learned, and it was hoped that these would increase until the Faith became a powerful world-religion. At this 'Nursery Colony', one girl would usually baby-sit while the other two went out delivering 'Mo Letters'.

Ruth told me that the children would start school at the age of two, at special Children of God schools. It seemed rather hard on them. A girl with no children told me that she hoped to have a baby soon, but made no mention of a husband. This recalled to my mind certain rumours that Children of God leaders take several wives and concubines. In this particular commune the leader seemed much-married in another sense, with no hanky panky. Psalms and Deuteronomy were nowhere to be seen, and everyone there seemed very clean-cut and well-to-do.

Ruth and her friend were very fashionably dressed, almost like young social workers – perhaps the result of successful prayer.

'Moses David is our Leader,' Ruth explained to me rather shyly, as if afraid that I would laugh at her great love. Instead I thanked them all for the coffee I had enjoyed, tickled a child called Solomon under the chin and went home well armed with 'Mo Letters'.

'Mo Letters' make curious reading. Many of them are in the form of cartoon strips, with Moses David taking the form of the 'Mo Lion' or 'The Mighty Mo', a wise, elderly lion dressed as a wizard and able to do magic. His usual disciple is 'Poorboy', a blond youth with big eyes, with whom the reader is meant to identify. Most of the 'Letters' condemn 'capitalism', picturing businessmen as being mysterious, sinister forces.

Parents, older people and bank clerk types are all assumed in the 'Letters' to be fanatical materialists, going purple with fury at any mention of God or the world of the spirit, and either driving 'Poorboy' away with threats or becoming converts and then facing the wrath of their former friends. Religion, it seems to be assumed, is a new discovery of Moses David's. Many young people *have* grown up in Britain with Godless parents, and thousands more with Churchless parents, so perhaps there is a grain of truth in the 'Mo Lion's' generalisation. However, my impression is that the redoubtable 'Lion' is impatient with family life. There is a case for this if a new religion demands a new life: and a convert to a higher faith can be expected to leave home and eventually begin a *new* family in different surround- ings. Monasteries and convents are another example, and they work well enough because *everyone* isn't expected to join them. Perhaps Moses David wants to break up the family as an idea, with 'Colonies' instead of households, and groups of converts of both sexes obeying a Leader, instead of having one married couple per home. Ironically enough, his 'Letters' refer to the Children of God as 'The Family'.

More serious 'Mo Letters' refer constantly to a Spirit World and make approving references to hypnotism. However the Spirits in this

World seem to be merely the erotic fantasies of Moses David. One picture of them shows angels with big bosoms! Conversion through seduction is a theme that occurs again and again, and the leaflets tell of Children of God discos and night clubs, though *I* haven't seen any. The girls I met all seemed to be perfectly decent, and probably don't know what Moses David is getting at. They do kiss everyone on the cheek and say 'We love you' in an American accent, but that seems to be just a formality. Outside Moses David's imagination, I would think that LSD had made more Children of God than sex.

'Look of Love' is one of the most explicit leaflets – collectors, please note! Girls are urged to 'go the limit' if it results in a conversion to Christ, Whose name looks very out of place among Mo's drivellings about the spirit-power of the sex urge. Moses David himself has actually boasted that after he looked into a German girl's eyes, the poor *fraulein* started frantically pleading to go to bed with him. I suppose men will tell such lies, but why in a religious pamphlet with holy names scattered about in it?

Other less sensational letters take a scientific pose, and explain that the heart must be made a vacuum so that God can enter, though how this is done is not explained. All the Children I met were harmless, but the eerie 'Mo Letters' tell another story. Who is Moses David? The only pictures of him I have seen, portrayed him as a mangy lion.

One day, perhaps, the American police will find out something that can close down some of the Faiths in the land where they are most deeply entrenched. California is almost a fountainhead of Faiths, perhaps because of the rich young people there. The Founders of the Faiths are obviously sincere in their belief that their mercenary behaviour stems from Divine Inspiration. Their many grown-up agents seem to be the lovers of organisation for its own sake.

After reading innumerable pamphlets of varying degrees of lunacy, I feel that if I never meet another mad-religionist again it will be too soon. The last one I met, Ruth Valiant, gave me the best advice – to soothe myself by reading the King James' Version of the Bible. I am now re-reading the Psalms, her friend's namesake.

Young people away from home have created a way of life from scratch, and as this way of life includes religion, it seems to me that religion is a part of human nature – we are a God-fearing animal. 'Scientific' philosophies on life, also of recent invention, are plainly akin to our mad religions, particularly Communism. 'Social and economic forces and the tide of history' are, in my opinion, a rather soulless way of saying 'God', and simply reassure the believer that Something is looking after him and the world.

'Supply and Demand' have brought the Faiths I have described into being, and if the religions are mad, it may be because the worshippers are mad also, mostly thanks to drug-taking. Still, many old-established world religions are distinctly strange, or even bloodthirsty. Their members may be perfectly nice people – the people can be better than the religion.

In Christianity we have a religion that is better than people. No one could live up to Christ's teachings save Christ Himself, but trying makes us better men. When everyone went to church, those who were genuinely spiritual had a ready-made religion, and one where they could be guided by the wisest of men.

Spirituality does not always go with brains, however, and thousands of young people who would once have been influenced by Christianity are now left floundering until they come into the orbit of a mad religion. Nothing the Church of England can do can get young people to attend the services in numbers. Even middle-aged people scarcely go to church, and those that do have no influence on their student children. University expansion is certainly the villain of the piece, and television programmes haven't helped by constantly showing a vicar as a figure of fun. Now the mere appearance of a vicar in a television series is enough to raise a gale of laughter, yet mad religions, a rich source of satire, are totally ignored. The Church seems to be weakening itself by taking on non-Christian attitudes and by forcing vicars of seventy and over, the ones who really believe in Christ, to retire. Younger clergymen, on the whole, only seem sincere when talking of secular things, and have accepted the false idea that Christianity and intelligence cannot go together.

If only everyone who complained of empty churches would go to church, the problem would be solved. It's heartening that empty churches are always *bemoaned* – even atheists seem disturbed and saddened to see them. Normal Britons are not as Godless as they seem at first sight, and even the 'materialists' everyone goes on about are vague Christians in part of their minds. They like church weddings, and their newspapers, the Daily Mirror and the Sun, have cartoon pages where it is assumed that angels sit on clouds and there is life after death. All people need is a lead from intellectuals, but instead orthodox religions are left to the stupid, and the imaginative are abandoned to the mad sects.

Some may think I have been a little unfair to these sects. An atheist would probably have been very tolerant, and would only have criticised the sects for asking for money. As I believe in one specific religion, Christianity, I feel I have the right to be intolerant towards madness and superstition, and I cry 'Out upon the Gurus!'

Were the faiths I have described true, I would have encouraged people to give them *even more* money! Our cathedrals and abbeys were not built from air. Even I would feel that to describe the Church of England as 'The True Church' would be overdoing it a bit, but as for Christianity as a whole, I would say this to the mass of Vague Believers: 'If you have to pretend that Christianity is true to make sense of the world, that is a sign that it *is* true! Be vague no more, call yourself Christians and we shall be a land of Christians, and the mad religions will dwindle away along with the mental confusion that caused them! Amen.'

THE END